MW01031600

The Medieval Achievement

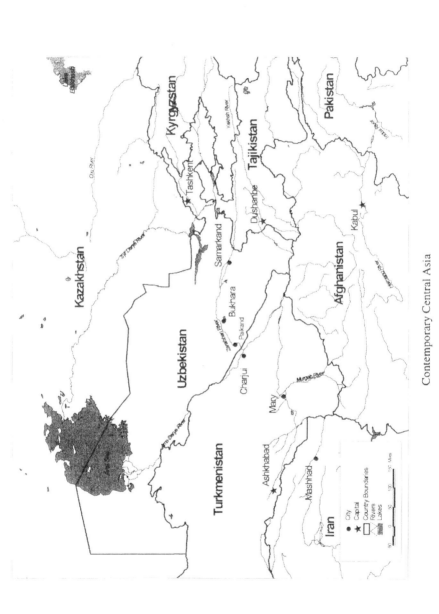

Contemporary Central Asia

Bibliotheca Iranica
Reprint Series No. 3

Bukhara

The Medieval Achievement

By Richard N. Frye

MAZDA PUBLISHERS
1997

Mazda Publishers
Since 1980
P.O. Box 2603
Costa Mesa, California 92626 U.S.A.
Homepage: www.mazdapub.com

Library of Congress Cataloging-in-Publication Data
Frye, Richard Nelson, 1920-
Bukhara: The Medieval Achievement/ by Richard N. Frye.
p. cm.—(Bibliotheca Iranica: Reprint Series No. 3)

ISBN:1-56859-048-2

(alk. paper)
1. Bukhara(Uzbekistan)—History. 2. Civilization, Iranian.
I. Title. II. Series.
DS876.F7 1996
958.7—dc21   96-40073
CIP

table of Contents

MAPS

Preface to Second Edition

After more than thirty years, and residence in Dushanbe, Tajikistan with many return visits to Bukhara, I find that the text of
the present work needs little change, although much could be
added. The results of archaeology and numismatic studies
have given us a more complete picture of Bukhara, especially
In pre-Islamic times. Even though the oasis of Bukhara was
settled in the first millennium B.C., if not earlier, the city of
Bukhara probably did not come into prominence until swamps
had been drained and canals dug on the delta of the Zarafshan
River about the beginning of the common era. Narshakhi
seems to be correct in stating that Paikand, where extensive
excavations have been conducted, and other villages of the
oasis, were older settlements than the town of Bukhara itself.

From coins we have names of rulers of Bukhara; the readings
of the obscure and difficult legends on the coins, unfortunately, are uncertain. The reader is referred to the additional
bibliography at the end of this preface, where the researches of
Rtveladze, Smirnova, Zeimal, and others, have shed light on
the ancient history of the oasis.

The Islamic period of Bukhara has not seen any new sources
or extensive studies, although the book by Numan Negmatov
summarizes our knowledge about the Samanids. Some items of
Information about Bukhara, especially its leading personages,
have been supplied by histories of Samarkand (Samarqand is
the Arabic form used in the book) and Nishapur.

There are certain remarks which should be made here about
various passages of our book. The form of a name of Bukhara,
Bumijkath may have been a misreading in some Arabic and
Persian texts for Numijkath, although the former is found

elsewhere in Central Asia, hence more common. On the other hand, Numijkath being the *lectio difficilior* might be preferable.

On p. 21 we do not know why Qutaiba b. Tughshada first supported Abu Muslim and then apparently thought Caliphal rule was over and joined an anti-Arab coalition. He may have hoped to regain some of his lost power and authority by playing off one Arab group against another.

Because of the long rule of Tughshada, and coinage, Olga Smirnova proposed that there was a Tughshada Jr. who ruled after his father of the same name, but this is uncertain On page 62, the difference between various Persian dialects and designations of languages have been further clarified by Gilbert Lazard (cf. Bibliography).

The ancestors of the slave soldiers of the Samanids (page 120) were the *chakir*s or mercenary guards of the Sogdian merchant princes, who left them to protect their families and possessions while the merchants went on long trading trips to China, Mongolia, or elsewhere.

Other remarks could be elaborated or more finely tuned, but the basic text of the book remains. It is intended for the general reader and students.

Richard N. Frye
August, 1996

Foreword

THE MAIN THESIS of the present work is that Bukhara, at the end of the ninth and in the tenth century, became the capital of the eastern Iranian cultural area, and thereby became the heir of a centuries-old tradition, independent of western Iran. At the same time Bukhara became the symbol of the new order—an Islamic Iran which had amalgamated the past with the religion and civilization brought by the prophet Muhammad. This development, called the New Persian Renaissance by some scholars, spread all over the Iranian Plateau and beyond. By some it has been decried as the re-action of Iranian "nationalism" against Arab Islam. I believe it was rather a successful attempt to save Islam, to release it from its Arab background and bedouin mores, by making of Islam a far richer, more adaptable, and universal culture than it had been previously. The Samanids showed the way to reconcile ancient traditions with Islam, a path followed by other peoples later in the far-flung corners of the Islamic world.

Bukhara did not lose its importance after the fall of the Samanids in 999; indeed it became a capital again under the Özbeks in the sixteenth century, and down to the Russian Revolution. But the great age of Bukhara was the tenth century when New Persian literature began to flower in the domain of the Samanids. After 999 Bukhara turned its face from Baghdad to Kashgar and then Qaraqorum. It became part of the southern outpost of the Central Asian Turkish extension rather than part of the northern frontier of the Iranian-Islamic world. Although Persian (or Tajiki) continues to be spoken by some in Bukhara down to the present, the Samanids were the last Iranian dynasty in Central Asia, and the Turkification of the land between the Oxus (Amu Darya) and Jaxartes (the present Syr Darya), in this book called Transoxiana, proceeded apace after 999. Another change was from the centralized bureaucratic state of the Samanids to the feudal decentralized kingdoms of the Qara-khanids (also called Ilik Khans or Al-i Afrasiyab), built on the Central Asian Turkish principle of double kingship. In a short book on Bukhara, however, we cannot discuss the problems of Central Asian steppe or nomadic customs, including political organization, much of which, in any case, is covered in other writings.

In my opinion a student of Transoxiana under Islam is faced with different problems and must use different methods in approaching his subject than his colleagues concerned with ancient Transoxiana, or with the history of Özbekistan since World War I. The ancient historian must utilize every scrap of evidence at his command, and he must exhaust every potentiality of a word in an inscription on a potsherd, or of an artifact from an archaeological excavation. He must employ the methods of comparative linguistics, anthropology, physical geography, and many other disciplines, to try to reconstruct the past. The historian of Samanid Bukhara and its surroundings must not neglect the information supplied by architecture, literature, and art, but his main task is to compare different versions of events found in the sources. Critical textual studies are his main occupation. The student of Soviet Bukhara must sift masses of information and countless records of economic, political, and social life in the city to build his history on a theme. His principal task is to select and reject information and then weave what he chooses into a consistent picture of a restricted period of time or a restricted subject, such as land tenure and cotton.

It is at once clear that an ancient history of Bukhara is impossible, whereas a general Islamic history, with many gaps, can be recovered. But then one must set limits to the story, determined by the purpose or theme. In our case it is the rise of the New Persian language and literature at the court of the Samanids and the changes in Transoxiana under the Qarakhanids. If our sources were more abundant and gave the information one would like, our task would be easier.

One problem of our sources is the lack of chronological exactitude and the utilization of previous works now lost. Thus in discussing the tenth century, sometimes a book written in the twelfth or thirteenth century will contain older and more reliable information than a similar work of the eleventh century. Most authors took their data from other books which they did not name, and sometimes they had very little concern with correct dates.

Most of the statements in this book can be documented by reference to specific sources. All references to authors or books are based on readings of the texts. The nature of the present book precludes footnotes, but the statements are based on an examination of relevant source material.

Although the sources leave much to be desired, one must

build upon them. I have tried to be consistent with names
and titles, not giving diacritical marks nor following a fully
unified system of transcription. In one case, for example, I
have followed an Arabic transcription, using *u, a* and *i* as
the only vowels, while in another Persian *o* or *e* has been
used, as well as *v* for *w*. This should cause no difficulty for
the student, while the general reader may welcome more
familiar forms of names. For quotations, I want to thank
the Yale University Press for allowing quotations from H.
Darke's translation of Nizam al-Mulk's *Siyasat Name* (New
Haven, 1960), the Oxford University Press for permission to
quote from D. Margoliouth's translation of Hilal al-Sabi,
under the title *The Experiences of Nations,* and the Harvard
University Press for the opening quotation from J. Boyle's
translation of Juvaini.

In writing this book I have tried to interpret data from the
sources in a wide framework. Many of our sources report
not what really happened, as Ranke would define history,
but what certain people believed to have happened, or even
what they thought should have happened. Following the
principle of simplicity consistent with the greatest amount
of data, I seek to explain the role of medieval Bukhara in the
wider contexts of the eastern Islamic world and the Turkification of Central Asia. Much has been omitted and I am
painfully conscious of the shortcomings of the present essay.
Yet I hope it may prove in some ways interesting, informa-
tive, and stimulating for certain problems.

I wish to thank Professor Omeljan Pritsak of Harvard for
reading the manuscript and offering suggestions, and Miss
Julie O'Neil and Miss Sue McElroy for typing it. I also wish

xii

Foreword

to thank Professor Stanford J. Shaw for reading the proofs. The staff of the University of Oklahoma Press has been very helpful in bringing this volume to print, for which they deserve high thanks.

RICHARD N. FRYE

Cambridge, Massachusetts
July 14, 1965

List of Illustrations

1. Wall painting from Varakhsha
2. Statuette of a woman from Varakhsha
3. Old Bukhara street scence.
4. Mosque of Magoki Attar
5. Close-up of mosque of Magoki Attar.
6. Minareh Kalan (12th century).
7. Plaster (*gach*) prayer niche ca. 11th century.
8. Metal mirror (Seljuk period)
9. Mausoleum of Samanids
10. Close-up of mausoleum of Samanids.
11. Carved wooden architrave of mosque (12th century?)
12. Page of Qur'an, dated 361 A.H./971 A.D.

BUKHARA
The Medieval Achievement

The almond groves of Samarqand,
Bokhara, where red lilies blow.
And Oxus, by whose yellow sand
The grave white-turbaned merchants go.

OSCAR WILDE

· 1 ·
The Ancient Oasis

"Aristobulus calls the river which flows through Sogdiana Polytimetus (most precious), a name imposed by the Macedonians."

STRABO, 518.

"IN THE EASTERN countries Bukhara is the cupola of Islam and is in those regions like unto Baghdad. Its environs are adorned with the brightness of the light of doctors and jurists and its surroundings embellished with the rarest of high attainments. Since ancient times it has in every age been the place of assembly of the great savants of every religion. Now the derivation of Bukhara is from *bukhar*, which in the language of the Magians signifies 'center of learning.' This word closely resembles a word in the language of the Uighur and Khitayan idolaters, who call their places of worship, which are idol temples, *bukhar*. But at the time of its foundation the name of the town was Bumijkath." So wrote the Persian historian Juvaini about 1260, long after the Mongols had taken and sacked Bukhara. The Golden Age of the city had passed but Bukhara never completely lost its importance even down to the end of the Tsarist empire in 1918.

Central Asia has always held a fascination for westerners, and the cities of Samarqand and Bukhara were twin jewels in that land of oases and deserts. People who live in well-watered forest lands have not experienced the wonder and

3

gratitude of men who have carved a small paradise from the sands of the desert, and have eked out even a precarious existence on an irrigated plot, ever on the defense against nature. For in Central Asia the line between the steppe and sown is sharply marked at the very edge of life-giving water, and to the nomad the oases must have seemed like paradise compared with the inhospitable deserts which he roamed.

Asiatic man at an early period of his existence, so the archaeologists tell us, seems to have descended from the hills, where he had learned to cultivate the soil and establish dwellings, into the more fertile river valleys. One of these valleys in Central Asia was created by the Zarafshan River flowing from the Pamirs, "the roof of the world," into the sands of the Kizil Kum desert.

There have been no discoveries of paleolithic settlements in the present-day oasis of Bukhara. This does not mean that there were no people of the Old Stone Age there, but only that so far nothing has been found. Since many layers of settlement have accumulated in the much irrigated and cultivated flat oasis, only deep excavations could be expected to produce very early remains. Inasmuch as elsewhere in Central Asia paleolithic tools have been found, one may assume that ancient settlements did also exist in the Bukharan oasis. A few Bronze Age objects attest the existence of settlements of the second millennium B.C. in our area, but not enough exploration or excavation has been carried out to give us a picture of the prehistory of Bukhara. We must content ourselves with early history and leave the earlier periods to future students of the prehistory of the area.

Central Asia entered the arena of history when Cyrus

established the far-flung Achæmenid empire. Yet the oasis of Bukhara is not mentioned in the Behistun inscription of Darius, nor is it in the list of countries under Persian rule by Herodotus. The religious book of the Zoroastrians, the Avesta, also fails to mention the area of Bukhara, so we may assume that it was included in the satrapy of Sogdiana, which is mentioned by all the above sources. The historians of Alexander the Great do not help us either, for we learn from Arrian and Quintus Curtius only that there were many settlements on the lower Polytimetus or Zarafshan River before it vanished in the sands, or at some period, it seems, into a lake called the Oxian Lake by Ptolemy. Archaeological evidence, fragmentary though it is, indicates the existence of irrigation canals and settlements in the oasis long before the coming of Alexander the Great. Unfortunately we have no literary sources relating to this early period.

Although we have no evidence, it would seem likely that the oasis of Bukhara was included in the Bactrian Greek kingdom founded by colonists and garrisons established by Alexander and the early Seleucid kings in eastern Iran. While the kings, Euthydemus, Demetrius, and others, may have exercised direct control over all of Sogdiana, it is more likely that the various oases of Central Asia maintained their autonomy even under nominal Bactrian Greek rule. Discoveries of Greco-Bactrian coins in Central Asia cannot serve as evidence for direct rule. On the other hand, there is no doubt that Hellenistic cultural influence was strong. The existence of sculptures and paintings from sites such as Airtam near Termez, Panjikant, and Varakhsha attest the important influence of Greek art in Central Asia in the two

5

centuries before the Christian era. The Greek influence in Central Asia probably paralleled Greek influence in northwest India, which later led to the Gandharan school of Buddhist art.

In the second century B.C. nomads from farther east invaded the land between the Oxus and Jaxartes rivers. Presumably they settled in the Bukharan oasis, imposing their rule on the local population. For the first time, we have Chinese sources telling about the lands of Central Asia. About 129 B.C. a Chinese ambassador called Ch'ang-ch'ien visited Central Asia and found that a people called the Yüeh-chih in Chinese texts had already occupied much of the land on the banks of the Oxus River. Later the Yüeh-chih conquered lands to the south of the Oxus, and one of their clans established a kingdom known in history, after the name of the clan, as the Kushan Empire. From the first to the fourth century A.D. the Kushan Empire was the dominant cultural as well as political power in Afghanistan and Central Asia.

Under the Kushans, Buddhism spread into Central Asia and to China. Now that inscriptions in the language of the Kushans have been found and partially deciphered (from Surkh Kotal in Afghanistan and elsewhere), we can better assess the important role of these successors of the Greeks in Central Asia. It was probably under the great King Kanishka (whose dates are uncertain but who probably flourished in the beginning of the second century A.D.) that the language of the Kushans was reduced to writing in a modified Greek alphabet. For we find both Greek and Kushan legends on Kanishka's early coins, whereas later in his reign Greek disappears. Perhaps more significant than

6

other cultural developments was the role of Kanishka and the Kushans in translating Buddhist writings into the Kushan language and then into Sogdian and Chinese. We may assume that many of the Sogdian and Chinese Buddhist documents from Chinese Turkistan were both translated from a Kushan original, since such common Buddhist terms as *saṃsāra*, "transmigration," *tathāgata*, "thus come," and *kleśa*, "impurity," in the Chinese and in Sogdian translations betray an origin from a third source, which was probably a school of translators of the Kushans. It was probably also under the Kushans that Buddhism came to the lands between the Oxus and Jaxartes rivers.

The importance of the Kushans in history has not been sufficiently emphasized, and as new archaeological discoveries enhance our knowledge of them, their role as cultural intermediaries between China, India, and the Near East will become more evident. In the oasis of Bukhara the distribution of potsherds of the Kushan period on many artificial mounds indicates a flourishing economy at this time. It is probably to this period that we can trace the earliest evidence of settlement on the site of the present city of Bukhara.

In excavations of one of the oldest mosques in the present city of Bukhara, Magoki Attar, the Soviet archaeologist V. A. Shishkin reached twelve meters below the surface, where sherds were found probably dating from the beginning of the Christian Era. The mosque of Magoki Attar may be identified with the Medieval mosque of Makh mentioned by Islamic authors, who say it was built on the site of a former fire temple. Since many sacred sites frequently con-

tinue their character even with changes in religion, witness
pagan temples changed into churches or churches into
mosques, the site of Magoki Attar, now in the heart of the
city, may be where a Buddhist monastery originally stood. So
we would have a mosque built upon a fire temple of some
local cult, which in turn was built upon a Buddhist *vihāra*.
These three religious strata might well correspond roughly
to the Muslim, Hephtalite, and Kushan eras in the history
of Bukhara.

A further indication that the above hypothesis is plausible
is the question of the names of Bukhara. In many Islamic
sources the original town of Bukhara is called Bumijkath
and an examination of medieval Islamic maps would lead
to the conclusion that Bumijkath was equivalent to the citadel, and that a stream or a canal separated Bumijkath from
the site of Makh, later Magoki Attar. So Bukhara as the
settlement around the temple of Makh, would have been
different from Bumijkath, and only later did the two merge.
It is impossible here to go into the reason for this hypothesis,
but it would clarify the notices on Bukhara in our sources,
especially the geographers.

It is interesting to observe that there is a town Bukhar in
the province of Bihar, India, and the origin of both names
is said to be from *vihāra,* the common name for a Buddhist
monastery. It is conceivable that the name Bukhara (in
Turkic languages *buqar*) is derived from *vihāra,* for it
would not be unusual to name a site after the most prominent structure in it. Furthermore, al-Khwarazmi, a writer
of the Samanid period, says *al-buhār* is an idol temple of

8

India. The name "Bukhara," however, is found relatively late in our sources. The earliest dated source in which the name occurs is the book of the travels of the Chinese Buddhist pilgrim Hsüan-tsang about 630 A.D. One may assume that the coins of the rulers of Bukhara, wherein the name appears, are earlier, but they are undated.

The coins are interesting copies of the silver pieces of the Sasanian ruler of Iran, Bahram V, who ruled *ca.* 421–39 A.D., and who presumably made conquests in Central Asia. The earliest coins of Bukhara of this type have a Middle Persian legend copied from the coins of Bahram, plus a legend in the local Bukharan language. The latter legend reads "Bukharan king," followed by either a proper name, Kana, or an appellation *kava,* "heroic, mighty," a local form of the name of the legendary, epic rulers before and contemporary with the prophet Zoroaster. The legend then could read "Bukharan king-emperor." Narshakhi the medieval historian of Bukhara, however, mentions a ruler of Bukhara called Kana who is presumably not a figment of the imagination, or the result of a later misreading of the coin legends, for on later coins the final *-a* vanishes. Much work needs to be done on the various types of coins from pre-Islamic Central Asia, but they too, I feel, will show the Kushan origins of later local dynasties.

One may suggest that the origins of Bukhara as an important city probably date from the late fifth or early sixth century A.D. when the Hephtalites were ruling large parts of Central Asia. After Bahram's defeat of the Hephtalites, Persian influence in Central Asia probably grew, as witnessed by the copying of his coins. To this same period archaeology assigns some major construction on the great walls around the oasis.

The great walls of Bukhara, amusingly called Kanpirak, "the old woman," were not unique in Central Asia. Antiochus I (281–261 B.C.) built a wall around the oasis of Merv, according to Strabo, while Samarqand, Shash (near Tashkent), and other oases also had walls. It is possible that the great walls of Bukhara, which extended for two hundred fifty kilometers around the oasis, were begun even before our era, but archaeological evidence is far from conclusive. The long walls enclosed the irrigated part of the oasis and they were undoubtedly a defense against the sands of the desert as well as against hostile nomads. Even today parts of the wall survive, especially in the eastern and southeastern areas of the oasis.

The walls were repaired and enlarged several times after the Arab conquests. Islamic sources tell us that a great restoration of the walls was begun in 782, which work lasted to 830. Under the prosperous rule of the Samanids the long walls were allowed to fall into ruins and they never again served as the great barrier which they were in pre-Samanid times. The walls of the city, of course, were maintained down almost to the present, and a medieval geographer, Istakhri, said that no other city in the eastern part of the Islamic world was as well fortified as Bukhara. Not only did the city have strong walls but the citadel, the seat of government, was exceptionally strong in its defenses.

To return to the Hephtalites, these invaders from farther east inherited the role of the Kushans, and seemingly also their language. Or one should say they adopted the Iranian language of Bactria used by the Kushans, for convenience called Kushan-Bactrian. It would be proper, I believe, to divide the history of the large east Iranian cultural area into a Kushan, followed by a later Hephtalite, period. This in no way excludes further subdivisions or other general views of the history of eastern Iran, but the lack of sources imposes a need for simplicity in any attempts to reconstruct the history. In the Persian epic by Firdosi the land of the Kushans seems to refer several times to the oasis of Bukhara, which would not be unexpected even later under Hephtalite rule.

We may assume that the Hephtalites ruled the oasis of Bukhara, as they did most of the east Iranian cultural area, from the middle of the fifth to the middle of the sixth century A.D. Although Turkic or Altaic elements may have existed among the Hephtalites, the main body of people seems to have been Iranian in language, and certainly in culture. In the medieval history of Bukhara by Narshakhi, we find a story which may report the downfall of the Hephtalite ruler of the oasis of Bukhara at the hand of the Turks about 565 A.D. The extract is not from the pen of Narshakhi but from another author called al-Nishapuri incorporated into the work of the former. The story tells us that before the city of Bukhara existed, the ruler of the entire area lived in the town of Paikand, which was southwest of the oasis near the Oxus River. A ruler called Abrui, or more probably Abarzi, so oppressed the people that they sought the aid of a Turkish ruler who captured and executed Abarzi. Much effort has been expended by scholars seeking to identify the various rulers mentioned in the story. Chinese texts are the main sources and they are rarely explicit in their accounts of this part of Central Asia so far from China. Since one of the royal family names of the Hephtalites was Warz, it is tempting to see in Abarzi the last Hephtalite ruler of the Bukharan oasis.

While the Turks exercised suzerainty over the Bukharan oasis, the real power seems to have rested in the hands of a local dynasty established probably in the fourth or fifth century following the breakup of the Kushan Empire into various principalities, at least north of the Oxus River. Again direct evidence for the long existence of the dynasty of the Bukharan oasis is not at hand, and we only hear of it from Arabic and Persian sources. In these sources the dynasty is known as the Bukhar Khudah (lord) dynasty. On the coins of these rulers, however, we find the Sogdian word for king γωβ, which is one detail among others indicating that the local language was a Sogdian dialect. The lords of Bukhara continued to rule in Islamic times, and we may assume that the dominion of the Arabs was similar to that of the Turks; both ruled through the local dynasty.

Stories which glorify the past of a city are frequently found in local medieval histories of various towns in Iran, and they must be carefully scrutinized before being used as sources. Stories of the pre-Islamic past which have no apparent aim or bias may be considered more trustworthy than tales which point up morals or unduly exalt a person or a place. Consequently, the information about pre-Islamic Bukhara found in Narshakhi's history, and repeated in other Islamic sources, can be accepted as substantially true unless proven to the contrary.

From several sources we learn that the capital Paikand was captured by Bahram Chobin, a general of the Sasanian king Hormizd IV, about 589. The adversary of Bahram could have been an important Turkish ruler or merely a local leader. The names Shaba and his son Parmudha (with variants), which appear in the sources, cannot be discussed here. There is much uncertainty about this period of history and speculation on details is not proper for our survey of Bukhara. In any case, after this time Paikand lost its importance and other towns of the oasis rose, among them Bukhara.

According to Nishapuri, in the book of Narshakhi, there was an ancient king of Bukhara called Makh after whom a later mosque in the city was named. Another king of Bukhara is mentioned on a silver vessel in the Hermitage Museum of Leningrad. The reading of the name is uncertain, but it could be read approximately as Dizoi. Narshakhi also mentions a ruler called Kana, whose name, as we mentioned, may appear on the coins. None of these names is certain and we can only suppose that such rulers did flourish in sixth and early seventh century Bukhara. We may be sure that there was a local dynasty in the city of Bukhara, but it is uncertain how much of the oasis was ruled by the lord of the city. It seems that other towns of the oasis had their own rulers, since we hear of the lord of the town of Vardana, in the north of the oasis, in Islamic sources. Furthermore, Narshakhi says that the town of Ramitin had been the capital of the oasis of Bukhara, and Varakhsha formerly had been the residence of rulers, all of which indicates various rulers as well as changes in the capital. By the time of the Arab conquests, however, the city of Bukhara was the principal town of the oasis.

13

· 2 ·
the Establishment of Islam

Put your face to the mihrab, *what is the gain?*
My heart is with Bukhara and the idols of Taraz.

RUDAKI

WHEN THE ARABS under the governor of Khurasan 'Ubaid-allah b. Ziyad arrived for the first time outside the walls of Bukhara in 674 they found a queen as regent in the city, for the king had recently died. The name of the queen, who apparently was an imposing person, was either Khtk or Qbkh, with the vocalization unknown. Various local conflicts make the story of the Arab conquests confusing and we cannot be sure of the sequence of events. It would appear that Bukhara paid tribute to the Arabs under 'Ubaidallah but was not occupied by the conquerors. Subsequent governors raided the lands across the Oxus River but their conquests were not consolidated mainly because of the civil war which broke out at the death of the Umayyad caliph Yazid b. Mu'awiya in 683. As a result Central Asia was free of the Arabs for a decade.

We do not know what happened in Bukhara. It is possible that the queen ruled Bukhara for more than thirty years, but it is more likely that the chronology is confused and that legends accumulated about the figure of the queen prolonging her reign. We hear of a certain Vardan Khudah,

14

or lord of the town of Vardana, who is also called Khnk, strangely similar to the name of the queen of Bukhara, as the chief opponent of the Arabs. A Bukhar Khudah, called Khnk, Khamik or Abu Shukr (father of Shukr) in the sources, may be identical with the lord of Vardana, or he may be another person entirely. Unfortunately the sources only mention these names and say nothing about them. It would seem that several rulers flourished in the oasis of Bukhara, and probably there were several claimants to the throne of the main city.

The raids of the Arab governor of Khurasan, Umayya b. 'Abdallah, from 692–97 proved ineffectual and the caliph 'Abd al-Malik placed Khurasan under the jurisdiction of Iraq with its strong and able viceroy, the famous Hajjaj b. Yusuf. The latter appointed an able lieutenant in Khurasan who finally conquered and occupied the lands to the north of the Oxus River. In 706 Qutaiba b. Muslim captured Paikand after a prolonged siege, and in 709 he took Bukhara. He also conquered Samarqand and extended Arab arms farther to the east than previous raids had even reached.

The rule of Qutaiba saw the establishment of Arab garrisons and the Islamic religion in Bukhara and in other cities of Transoxiana. Our sources tell us that Qutaiba assigned certain parts of the city of Bukhara to various Arab tribes, which gave a unity and strength to the conquerors in their occupation. Hajjaj and Qutaiba were both very able men, and their diplomacy, both in making compromises with local dynasties and enrolling many non-Arabs in the army, was the principal reason for the success of Islam in

Central Asia. This policy later caused great opposition among some Arabs and was a factor which led to Qutaiba's death at the hands of his opponents in 715.

Qutaiba established a mosque in Bukhara and quartered his garrison troops in the city. Various sources tell us that this action made of Bukhara not only an important Muslim military base but also laid the foundation for its role as a center of Islamic learning. Narshakhi tells us that Qutaiba offered a reward of two *dirhems* to everyone who came to the great mosque of Bukhara on Fridays. We may conclude that in Bukhara, as elsewhere, the lower classes flocked to Islam and the number of Muslims increased. This does not mean that only the poor people converted to Islam; rather the aristocracy was less inclined to do so.

Qutaiba established Arab military governors in towns in Transoxiana whose main duty was to oversee the collection of taxes and insure the common defense against enemies. Usually the local dynasts continued to exist side by side with the Arab governors, and in Bukhara the dynasty of the Bukhar Khudahs continued to flourish. It is not certain that Tughshada, the lord of Bukhara, was confirmed on his throne by Qutaiba, over his opponent the ruler of Vardana who had pretensions to the throne of Bukhara, but Tughshada was surely supported by Qutaiba. The form of his name is open to discussion, for we have Chinese as well as Arabic variants, but here we shall retain the spelling accepted in general secondary works. It seems that Tughshada ruled Bukhara for more than thirty years. Narshakhi says he ruled thirty-two years (707–39) and was installed originally by Qutaiba.

Narshakhi tells an interesting story about Tughshada some time after the death of Qutaiba. It seems that about 730 A.D. (the date is uncertain) an attempt was made by Arab missionaries to convert more inhabitants of Central Asia to Islam, and they were most successful. Tughshada complained to the governor of Khurasan that many people had accepted Islam only to avoid paying the tax levied on non-Muslims. The governor wrote to his representative in Bukhara to arrest the new Muslims and turn them over to Tughshada. The latter executed many of them and sent others as prisoners to the governor of Khurasan. Although the exact details of this story may not be accurate, the overall story, also told in several Arabic histories, shows how the problems of conversion to Islam and the taxes plagued the government officials, both local and Arab. As usual, revenues to the state took precedence over everything else.

To return to Qutaiba, the conversion of local people to Islam provided him with auxiliary troops side by side with the Arabs. The number of these non-Arab troops, called *mawali* or clients, increased, and they very much helped to consolidate and maintain Arab rule. The Arabs probably used Persian as the *lingua franca* with their Iranian subjects in Central Asia, as well as in Iran, which would help to account for the spread of the New Persian tongue to lands where Sogdian and other languages or dialects were spoken locally.

After the death of Qutaiba the position of the Arabs deteriorated and the chronicle of revolts and battles becomes monotonous. Bukhara remained in Arab hands, although other localities were from time to time fully independent.

Many embassies to the court of China from various dynasts of Central Asia, seeking help against the Arabs, are recorded in the Chinese annals. Even Bukhara requested aid from China together with other states in 718 or 719. It would seem that Tughshada played a double game encouraging other princes to organize resistance to the Arabs with Chinese or Turkish aid, but then affirming his loyalty to the Arabs when the latter were strong. The changing policies of the Arabs themselves in the East, reflecting the central authority of the Umayyad caliph in Damascus, did not serve to reconcile the natives.

Chinese sources tell us that the king of Bukhara sent his brother to the court of China in 726 offering submission. This was probably part of the general revolt against the Arabs after several defeats of the latter at the hands of the Turks, or more precisely the Türgish from the north and east of Transoxiana. In 728 Bukhara and most of Transoxiana, save Samarqand and a few small localities, were free from Arab rule. Two years later Bukhara capitulated to an Arab army, but somehow Tughshada managed to remain in power. The Arabs had to fight the Türgish with their local allies for several years, and on one occasion the Muslims in Bukhara were besieged by the Türgish. Fighting continued until 737 when the Türgish withdrew from Transoxiana because of internal problems.

The new governor of Khurasan, and the last of the Umayyad appointees, Nasr b. Sayyar, was able to repeat the conquests of Qutaiba. He did it more by diplomacy than by fighting, for he had been in Central Asia from the time of Qutaiba and was a well seasoned veteran with a good understanding of local problems. Nasr wisely issued a decree of amnesty to rebels against Arab rule and he established acceptable terms of taxation for the inhabitants. On his return trip from a successful expedition to the Jaxartes River, Nasr met Tughshada and the Arab governor of Bukhara in Samarqand. Both Narshakhi and Arabic sources tell how two nobles of Bukhara complained of Tughshada and Wasil b. 'Amr the Arab governor of Bukhara before Nasr. Since Nasr was very friendly with Tughshada he was not inclined to listen to their complaints, whereupon they stabbed Tughshada and Wasil and were themselves killed. This occurred probably in 739 and Nasr confirmed the son of Tughshada as lord of Bukhara.

By the time of the death of Tughshada, Arab rule was firmly established in Bukhara. It is interesting to mention the change in the government accounting system from Pahlavi to Arabic under Nasr b. Sayyar. First he was ordered by the caliph to dismiss any non-Muslim from the ranks of government functionaries in Khurasan. Then he changed the official language to Arabic, presumably from previous Middle Persian or Pahlavi, although the use of Parthian in Khurasan is not to be dismissed as anachronistic. Sogdian was probably the "official language" of Transoxiana, while Kushan-Bactrian in Greek letters may have been used in the area of present-day Afghanistan. One might say that at the end of Umayyad rule in Bukhara the process of Arabicization and Islamization had established supremacy over the cultural and social life of the city. This does not mean that Zoroastrians, Jews, Christians, or even Manichaeans ceased to exist in Bukhara. Rather Islam was secure and Arabic became the language not only of state but of learning after this time. It is probable that Tughshada was some sort of a local Zoroastrian rather than a Muslim, for, according to Narshakhi and others, when he died his servants removed his flesh from his bones and brought them to Bukhara. The bones were probably preserved in a box called an *astodan*. Since burial customs are not reliable guides to the religion of the deceased, we cannot say more about Tughshada's faith or about the religious situation in Bukhara in regard to the non-Muslims.

The successor of Tughshada was his son Bishr, according to some sources, or another son Qutaiba, according to others. Perhaps they were the same, or the latter succeeded Bishr after a short rule. In any case, by their names at least the successors of Tughshada professed Islam. Qutaiba, of course, was named after the great Arab general.

We cannot here discuss the 'Abbasid revolt and the various inter-tribal conflicts of the Arabs in Khurasan. I believe that the tribal conflicts, important though they were in the rise of the 'Abbasids, have been overemphasized. The fall of the Umayyads and the advent of the 'Abbasid Caliphate involved much more than the quarrels of northern and southern Arab tribes. We must confine our attention, however, to Bukhara.

When Abu Muslim, the 'Abbasid leader in Khurasan, forced Nasr to evacuate the province in 748 Bukhara was left to its own devices. An Arab called Sharik b. Shaikh al-Mahri gained possession of the city of Bukhara in 750 and raised the standard of the Shi'ites, the partisans of the family of 'Ali. Abu Muslim as a result sent an army against Bukhara, whose lord, Qutaiba b. Tughshada, joined the 'Abbasid forces as they pressed the siege of the city. Narshakhi writes that the followers of Qutaiba were from the villas outside of the city and there were no Arabs among them, whereas in the city were Arabs as well as natives. It seems that the partisans of Sharik were the city classes whereas the aristocracy supported Qutaiba b. Tughshada, who was a partisan of Abu Muslim. Fighting was fierce and cruel but the death of Sharik opened the way to victory for the 'Abbasid forces. Some of the city was burned during the struggles and many leaders of the revolt of Sharik were executed after the capture of the city.

The 'Abbasid armies, after the capture of Bukhara, pacified the rest of Transoxiana, and even a Chinese army was defeated by the Arabs in 751. Probably some of the local princes hoped for Chinese aid against the 'Abbasid forces, for we learn of embassies to China from several local states, including Bukhara, during this period. It seems it was in the violent reaction of Abu Muslim against this anti-'Abbasid coalition that the lord of Bukhara, Qutaiba, was put to death in 751 or 752. Several sources say that Abu Muslim killed him because he apostatized from Islam. This may be true but the political circumstances should not be overlooked.

With the establishment of the 'Abbasid Caliphate, the lands of the east, Khurasan and Transoxiana, assumed a greater role in the destinies of the Islamic world. The shift in the capital from Damascus to Baghdad was a sign of the change. Iranian influence now became strong at the court in Baghdad, and in the provinces one may assume that the process of mixing and assimilation of Islamic and Iranian

21

cultures proceeded apace. The history of Transoxiana under the early 'Abbasids is no longer the story of Arabs against the local inhabitants, but of Muslim political or religious rebels against the central authority. In the first decade after the establishment of the 'Abbasid Caliphate several embassies from the king of Bukhara to China are mentioned in Chinese annals. Thereafter they ceased as both China and the local principalities of Central Asia declined in importance for the affairs of Transoxiana.

The Bukhar Khudah from about 751–57 was probably one Sukan, another son of Tughshada. This name may stand for the Turkish name Arslan, since the latter is mentioned in Chinese sources, but it is dubious. Nothing is recorded about his reign, but under his successor Bunyat (*ca.* 757–82), also a son of Tughshada, there were a number of revolts in Bukhara. At the beginning of his rule the Arab governor of Bukhara was executed by his superior, the governor of Khurasan, because of Shi'ite activities. In fact Shi'ite partisans in the city plagued the central authorities, but they were not alone in causing trouble. In 777 the Kharijites, an ultra-conservative but activist Islamic sect under one Yusuf al-Barm, revolted at Bukhara. He was soon caught and executed, but other rebels were ready to take his place.

The most significant revolt was that of a non-Muslim called Muqanna', which lasted from about 776 to 783 and gained many adherents in the villages of the Bukharan oasis. The city, however, remained under 'Abbasid control as a center of operations against the rebel. Much has been written about Muqanna', since he seems to have preached a social doctrine of communism, even the sharing of wives, and he held to a belief in metempsychosis, declaring he was a reincarnation of previous prophets and even of Abu Muslim. His followers were called the wearers of "white raiments," and they undoubtedly included many political and social as well as religious dissidents. Several years of fighting in the oasis of Bukhara as well as elsewhere in Transoxiana were necessary before Muqanna' was killed and his followers scattered.

From Narshakhi we learn that Bunyat showed partiality for the followers of Muqanna' and consequently was executed by order of the caliph Mahdi about 782. There is considerable confusion in the account of his death by Narshakhi, who claims that Sukan was also killed by order of the caliph. The sequence of rulers and the chronology being confused, one can only surmise the history. Since both rulers were said to have been killed in Varakhsha, which has been excavated by Soviet archaeologists, we may assume that the court of the rulers of Bukhara, at least under Islam, was at Varakhsha rather than in the city. This observation fits with many scattered literary notices as well as the results of excavations, where remains of wall paintings and elaborate stucco decorations attest to the splendor if not to the power of the local dynasts of Bukhara.

Narshakhi tells us that Bunyat was seated in his castle in Varakhsha drinking wine with his companions when he saw horsemen rapidly approaching. He was wondering if they had come from the caliph, when they arrived and without saying a word drew their swords and cut off his head. Thus ended the last of the lords of Bukhara, for his descendants held no power and even their land owning and possessions were greatly reduced. Their coins, however, were longer lasting than the influence of the dynasty.

The coinage of medieval Bukhara is important because of the role it played as the basis for the silver coinage of most of Transoxiana in Islamic times. The coins are essentially the same over a long period of time, varying only in legends and in metallic composition. The reverse of the coins shows a fire altar flanked on both sides by a figure, while the obverse shows a crowned prince facing right, and it is clear that the figure is copied from Bahram V (421-39), the Sasanian ruler. We may reasonably assert that the earliest silver coins of Bukhara *of this type* date from some time after 439, but how much later? Actually, an examination of the coins of Yaz-dagird II (438-57) and Balash (484-88) reveals a close simi-larity in the crowns of the three rulers and in the general types of the coins. One might suggest that the series of "Bukhar Khudah" coins began sometime before the sixth century, although it cannot be excluded that Narshakhi is correct when he says that the first ruler to strike such coins in Bukhara was a ruler called Kana in the fourth decade of the seventh century. We can hardly believe that no other coinage existed earlier, although again Narshakhi may be correct in his statement that previously only coins of Khwa-razm (and other cities of Central Asia?) were current in the oasis of Bukhara.

When the Arabs arrived the "Bukhar Khudah" coins were in common use, and the conquerors continued to strike them. The development from a Pahlavi legend to an all Bukharan legend to an all Arabic legend can be traced on the coins.

The Establishment of Islam

The changes, I believe, mirror the evolution of Bukhara from a local center under strong Sasanian influence to an important pan-Islamic center.

Although, as we have mentioned, there is still uncertainty about the correct reading of the Bukharan inscription on the coins, their widespread currency in 'Abbasid times is not in dispute. The research of a Soviet numismatist, E. A. Davidovich, has convincingly shown that the three kinds of "Bukhar Khudah" coins in circulation in various parts of Central Asia in the ninth and tenth centuries differed in rate of exchange. The coins, called Musayyabi, Ghitrifi, and Muhammadi in the sources, although similar in appearance, differed in the content of metal, probably in a descending order given above. The Ghitrifi was especially used in the Bukhara area, and the Muhammadi in Sogdiana. All of these "silver" coins, or *dirhems,* were impure, and their rates of exchange with the purer silver *dirhems* of the rest of the caliphate varied considerably from time to time. In any case, Bukhara, it seems, provided the coin type for the local coinage of Transoxiana even late into Islamic times, an indication of the growing importance of the city.

To return to the story of Bukhara, the century after the execution of Bunyat to the coming of Isma'il Samani in 874 is relatively uneventful compared with the earlier history. From 806–10 Nasr b. Sayyar's grandson, called Rafi' b. Laith, revolted. At the beginning he captured Samarqand. The people of Bukhara and other cities in Central Asia supported him against the 'Abbasids, but the accession of the caliph Ma'mun brought a reconciliation and an end of the revolt. Both in the revolt of Muqanna' and of Rafi' the help

of Turkish troops from the north and east to the rebels fore-
shadowed the later extensive Turkish migrations into the
Near East. The nomads were a constant threat to the security
of the oases, such that the government had to propose serious
measures for defense against them. The great walls of the
Bukharan oasis were rebuilt during the period under discussion, while other oases of Transoxiana were also fortified.

The walls of the oasis of Bukhara, called Kanpirak, protected most of the settled areas. Narshakhi says that every
year the expenditure of much money and a large labor force
were required to care for the wall. Undoubtedly the main-
tenance of the walls was a heavy burden on the people, even
if the ramparts did protect the oasis from raiding Turkish
nomads who previously came without warning and plundered villages, carrying away captives. It seems clear that
the oases of Central Asia required constant protection against
nomadic raiders, hence the need for thick walls everywhere.
Houses were built with thick walls surrounding the yards
and gardens as well as the dwellings, while narrow, winding
streets gave more security to the inhabitants. Furthermore,
the entire city had strong walls, and the seat of government in
the citadel was also strongly fortified.

In Bukhara the citadel was a raised area dominating the
city, containing a prison and a mosque and government
offices as well as the residence of the ruler. From archaeological surveys we learn that clay, stucco, and wood were
the main building materials. Actually brick rather than stone
was the principal building material all over the Iranian
world, from Mesopotamia to India and China. Probably the
decorated cornices, the stucco decorations, and the wall paint-

ings of the castle of the Bukhar Khudahs in Varakhsha were as elaborate and lovely as any in the neighboring Sasanian empire. Soviet excavations in Khwarazm, in Sogdiana, and elsewhere are beginning to reveal the great extent and richness of the pre-Islamic culture of Transoxiana, an important center of a particular civilization, and not just an extension of Sasanian Iran to the northeast. Undoubtedly there was great influence from Iran, as can be seen in the art, the coinage, and, of course, the New Persian language which developed in Central Asia, but the "feudal" culture of local princes was distinctive.

It was probably in the feudal eastern Iranian area that the all-Persian epic, versified by Firdosi, had its origin. Certainly the geographic localities, insofar as they can be established in an epic, refer primarily to eastern Iran. From the accounts of Chinese Buddhist pilgrims, it is clear that Buddhism had retreated in Transoxiana at the expense of some sort of Zoroastrianism. Inasmuch as Bukhara did not belong to the Sasanian Empire, it would be hazardous to identify the prevailing faith in Central Asia with the state religion of the Sasanians. Narshakhi implies that the inhabitants of Bukhara had been idol worshippers before they became fire worshippers. From scattered brief notices in the sources, one might infer that the majority of the population of the oasis followed a local cult, in which the mythical or epic figure of Siyavush played an important role. There is no reason to doubt the statements of several Arabic and Persian sources that dirges on the death of Siyavush were well known and sacrifices were performed over his grave near Bukhara.

The pomp and splendor of the princely courts of Central

Asia may be surmised from the wall paintings found by archaeologists at Varakhsha in the oasis of Bukhara, at Panjikant east of Samarqand, and at Balalyk Tepe north of Termez. Although they do not date from the same period, they all reflect the pre-Islamic culture of Central Asia. Elaborate costumes, revealing a highly developed textile industry, special flat drinking bowls, and daggers or swords bound to the waists, are characteristic of the wall paintings. We know that the Sasanian kings were wont to bestow silver drinking bowls on favorites, and here on the wall paintings we find similar bowls painted. They must have been inconvenient for drinking wine, but fashions and styles have frequently gone against comfort or utility.

We may assume that bards attended the local aristocracy when they met for an evening of pleasure. Fragments of a story of Rustam in Sogdian have been found which are different from the tale of Rustam in Firdosi's *Shah Name*. Perhaps Rustam, who is an important hero if not the main actor of the Persian epic, was originally a Saka prince from Central Asia. Surely stories about him flourished in the oasis of Bukhara not only before but after Islam.

From Narshakhi and others we learn that the aristocracy of Bukhara for the most part resided in villas outside of the city. Here they held their minor courts surrounded by their guards or servants called *chakir*. While the lack of unity among the Central Asian princes and aristocracy contributed to Arab victories, the feudal character of society made Central Asia difficult to rule. Once the imperial Sasanian armies were destroyed the Arabs overran Iran, but Central Asia proved a much more difficult area to rule, and Islam itself and Islamic culture changed before they completely triumphed in the eastern part of the caliphate.

Islam gave the entire Near East, including Transoxiana, a unity which it had not enjoyed since the Achaemenids and Alexander the Great. Furthermore, even more than Hellenism, Islam provided a spiritual and cultural bond which has endured to the present day. Bukhara under its local lords had been an important city center, but under Islam it became a world city known to people as far away as Spain and China. The golden age of the city coincided with the rise of the New Persian language and literature and with the ecumenical development of Islam, and Bukhara played an important role in both.

· 3 ·

The Rise of the Samanids

Long live Bukhara! Be thou of good cheer!
Joyous towards thee hasteth our Amir.
The moon's the prince, Bukhara is the sky;
O sky, the moon shall light thee by and by.

RUDAKI

(Translation of E. G. Browne)

THE CITY OF BUKHARA expanded considerably in the ninth century. Whereas in pre-Islamic times the market place had been outside of the city walls, by the ninth century not only it, but also many suburbs were included in the city, together with the ancient, original town called the *shahristan*. The citadel or *arg* did not correspond to the *shahristan* but was separate from it. The entire city by the end of the ninth century had two walls, an inner and an outer one, each with eleven gates, the names of which are given by Arabic geographers as well as by works in Persian.

During the rule of the Umayyads and early 'Abbasids, Bukhara was under the jurisdiction of the extensive province of Khurasan with its capital at Merv. When the governors or *amirs* of Khurasan changed their residence from Merv to Nishapur, under Tahir about 821 if not earlier, it seems the oasis of Bukhara received an administration separate from the rest of Transoxiana, and directly responsible to the governor of Khurasan at Nishapur. It is interesting that the Bukhar Khudahs maintained a villa or palace in Merv at the time that the latter was the capital of Khurasan, probably for reasons of commerce as well as politics.

The growing commercial importance of Bukhara is also revealed by the sources. Of special importance in the medieval Islamic world were textiles, and fragments of silks and other cloth from this period indicate the highly developed state of design and weaving. The oasis of Bukhara was famous for its cloth Zandaniji, which was named after the village of Zandana, several pieces of which have been identified in contemporary museums. Narshakhi says that this cloth was exported to India and Iraq since it was highly esteemed by the aristocracy everywhere. The same author also says that the tax of Bukhara was collected by agents of the caliph in Baghdad not in money but in cloth and rugs. The geographer Maqdisi, who wrote in Arabic, gives the names of various textiles from Bukhara as well as from the neighboring towns, all of which were exported, thus bringing revenue to the oasis.

The irrigation system of Bukhara should be mentioned, for here as elsewhere in the Orient water was the life blood of the city. For the oasis of Bukhara the Zarafshan River provided water to such an extent that the river had no outlet, being completely utilized by the many canals which led water from it to the fields. In ancient times the river had drained into a lake or swamp, which later vanished because of irrigation. The famous system of underground irrigation tunnels, called *kariz* in Central Asia, was not necessary in the oasis of Bukhara since the water was near at hand and quickly utilized. Narshakhi tells us that every stream in the oasis except one was dug by man, hence all were in origin irrigation canals. The canals of the oasis, like the gates of the walls, were known to the geographers, who give their names. The fruit of Bukhara was famous and was exported to Merv, according to the geographer Yaqut. Certainly the fertility of the soil well rewarded the attention and labor devoted to it.

As the city grew in importance its role in the political events of the eastern part of the caliphate became more significant. Members of the family of the old Bukhar Khudahs received positions in other parts of the caliphate. Tabari, the great Persian historian writing in Arabic, mentions an 'Abbas b. Bukhar Khudah as an important caliphal official in 811, and in 836 another member of the family, Muhammad b. Khalid, is mentioned as a general fighting a rebel called Babak in Azerbaijan province. The same person became governor of Armenia in 838 after the defeat of Babak, and Armenian sources refer to him as the Bukhar Khudah. It should be noted that the family continued to exercise some influence at Bukhara, since Khalid b. Bunyat was considered the successor of his father Bunyat, even though his actual power must have been small.

The aristocracy or *dihqans* were the backbone of society and owned most of the land. We have noted that they were probably the most loath to give up their old customs and religion in favor of Islam. Indeed the progress of Islam in Central Asia was slower than we have hitherto thought. A fifteenth century history of Bukhara by an author called Mullazade (the priest's son) tells us that as late as 814 Muslims were martyred in Bukhara at the hands of infidels. Such occurrences must have been rare, but it is possible that certain parts of the city had fewer Muslims than others and consequently clashes may have occurred. There cannot have been any threat to Islam by this date and the advent of a new dynasty, the independent Tahirid governors of Khurasan, presaged a new era in Islamic history.

Tahir was an influential general of the caliph Ma'mun and in 821 he became governor of Khurasan. His son succeeded him (822–28), and thereby a dynasty was established. Other members of the family held important posts in other parts of the caliphate such as Egypt, so the dynasty had more than local importance. The Tahirids were legally only governors of Khurasan appointed by the caliphs, and they paid a fixed amount of taxes to the central government. Nonetheless they were in fact independent sovereigns. Since the interests of the Tahirids and the caliphs usually coincided, there was little reason for conflict. The Tahirids were staunch Sunnis and attacked Shi'ites and other heretics in their realms with the approbation of the authorities in Baghdad.

What interests us, concerned with Bukhara, is the role of the Tahirids in the formation of the New Persian language and literature. The consensus has been that the Tahirids represented national Persian aspirations and under them Persian developed as an opposition to Arabic, which was the language of the conquerors. I believe this position must be modified. If we examine the reigns of the Tahirids we find no evidence that these rulers favored Persian over Arabic. Quite the contrary; several of the Tahirid rulers were good poets and writers in Arabic. Undoubtedly they knew both languages, but Arabic was the official language of the state.

This does not mean that Persian was not written in Arabic

characters at the time of the Tahirids. There is every reason
to believe that attempts to write Persian with Arabic letters
were made before the ninth century. The rapid spread of
Arabic as a literary language all over the Islamic world
probably acted as a catalyst on the Persian language. Copying
Persian texts in the Arabic alphabet rather than the archaic,
inefficient Pahlavi system of writing must have appeared
reasonable to many cultured Persians. The scribal class in
the 'Abbasid caliphate was both Muslim and predominantly
non-Arab in the eastern part of the empire. What would be
more natural than experiments by this group to write the
local spoken language in the official script to which they
were accustomed? Although no manuscripts of Sogdian
written in the Arabic alphabet have survived, probably because of the rather rapid decline of the language, we do have
books in the Khwarazmian language with Arabic alphabet.

The fact that some early poems in New Persian do exist
which are Middle Persian in form, to be scanned by accent
or mere number of syllables and not in long and short syllables, indicates that these poems are simply Middle Persian
poems written in the Arabic script. Between 800 and 900
A.D., however, Persian poems are recorded which do not
differ from Arabic poems with their system of long and short
syllables. This would indicate that the criterion for the creation of a New Persian literature is really the Arabic form
of poetry plus other influences from Arabic, not just the
alphabet. In other words the creation of a New Persian
literature, beginning with poetry, as expected, is connected
with the Islamization or Arabicization of Persian culture.
It is, I believe, more accurate to speak of the Islamization

34

than of the Arabicization of Persian, since by the middle of the ninth century Classical Arabic had become a world language and not just the vehicle of bedouin Arabs with their limited horizons. Furthermore, Islam was no longer identical with Arab customs and beliefs but was an ecumenical culture and civilization as well as a religion.

The process of fusion between Arabic and Persian was developing throughout the ninth century in Bukhara as well as Nishapur, and there is no evidence that the Tahirids made Nishapur a center of New Persian poetry and literature by any policy, covert or declared. The successors of the Tahirids in Transoxiana, the Samanids, however, were patrons of New Persian even though they too fostered Arabic in their domains.

Most scholars now believe that Saman was a petty prince or *dihqan* in a town of the same name near Termez, who on converting to Islam saw his star rise. Concerning his son Asad, nothing is reported in the sources, but the grandsons attained high offices after supporting Ma'mun in the suppression of the revolt of Rafi' b. Laith. About 820 one son Nuh was appointed governor of Samarqand, Ahmad in Ferghana, Yahya in Shash or modern Tashkent, while the fourth brother Ilyas was given Herat.

The Samanids seem to have been a clannish family, with the eldest male person succeeding to headship of the entire family. When Nuh, the eldest of the four brothers, died in 842, the next in seniority, Ahmad, took over the family and sent his eldest son Nasr to represent himself in Samarqand. When Ahmad died in 864, his son Nasr became the family chief, but maintained his seat of government in Samarqand.

According to W. Barthold, the authority for Central Asia during this period, the ninth century saw the complete conquest of all of Transoxiana by Islam. For example, the local dynasty of Usrushana, in the present Ferghana valley, was subdued in 822 and the ruler constrained to adopt Islam. Although the territories ruled by the Samanid brothers were wealthy in natural resources, the entire area was still under the jurisdiction of the Tahirids who alone struck caliphal silver coins *(dirhems)*. The Samanids could only mint copper coins *(fels)*. This, of course, was in addition to local coinages.

The consolidation of Central Asian lands under the Samanids was to lead to their independence as soon as the Tahirids lost their power. Meanwhile the Samanids were not idle. We have mentioned the work of fortification of the oases in this period against the Turkish nomads, which was on the whole a Samanid undertaking. The Turks, of course, were no strangers to Transoxiana, even from the pre-Islamic period. There probably was an infiltration of Turks at all periods, and the Turkish guards or mercenaries at the caliphal courts are well known. About 840 Nuh b. Asad attacked the Turkish ruler of Isfijab, north of present-day Tashkent. Nuh was victorious and occupied the city, building a long wall around the suburbs as well as the city itself as a defense against the nomads. The Turkish trickle into the Islamic world was to become a flood at the end of Samanid rule, but it was a threat at all times.

The fall of the Tahirid dynasty in 873, with the capture of Nishapur by a bandit chief called Ya'qub b. Laith from Seistan, changed the political situation in eastern Iran and Central Asia. The early Tahirids, according to many later authors, were exemplary rulers who fostered learning as well as irrigation and the well-being of all their subjects. Indeed 'Abdallah b. Tahir is credited with the compilation of a treatise on the legal aspects of irrigation, the "book of canals." The later Tahirids, however, according to a time-honored Oriental tradition, abandoned good works for actions leading to their own pleasure and amusement, which opened the way to an easy conquest by the enemy.

Ya'qub was a coppersmith who formed a band of *ghazis* or "warriors for Islam." These were usually little more than outlaws in spite of the religious aspects of their struggles in the "holy war" against infidels. Ya'qub became the leader of his band and won fame and followers in expanding his power on the frontiers of India. Although of low-class origins, he soon was able to overthrow some of the aristocratic leaders in Kirman, Balkh and elsewhere, finally, as mentioned, capturing Muhammad, last of the Tahirids in Nishapur.

Many writers have described Ya'qub as a proletarian rebel, and the sources do tell how he confiscated the property of many aristocrats. There was no great change in society or in the feudal basis of land holding, however, during the reigns of Ya'qub and his brother and successor 'Amr. Indeed the traditional power of the *dihqans* was firmly established, especially in eastern Iran and Central Asia. Nonetheless the victories of Ya'qub shook the authority of the caliph who had established a working relationship with the Tahirids.

In Transoxiana after 873 the Tahirids tried to maintain a semblance of authority. In the following year a Tahirid called Husain came to Bukhara from Khwarazm and after a siege captured the city. At first successful, he was then obliged to flee, leaving everything behind him. Riots followed, and one may assume that followers of Ya'qub b. Laith contested control of the city with partisans of others. At this time there is some evidence that dissident Muslim heretics called Kharijites were strong in the city, probably with a party which may have controlled Bukhara for a time. Under the confused circumstances some leading citizens of Bukhara appealed to Nasr b. Ahmad, the Samanid ruler of Samarqand, to send someone to rule them. Nasr sent his younger brother Isma'il, who became the real founder of the Samanid dynasty.

Isma'il was born in Ferghana in 849, but nothing is known of his early life before he came to Bukhara. The sources tell us that, since he did not come with an army, he was unwilling to enter the city without strong assurance of support from the leading citizens. Once this was secured, he entered the city to the delight of the population and took control of the government. This was late in 874 or early in 875. Bukhara had at last found a worthy governor.

Isma'il was ushered into the city of Bukhara by the populace, which scattered coins over his head, an ancient custom which spread even to the Tsars of Muscovy in later times. In the same year that Isma'il entered Bukhara, his brother Nasr received a document from the caliph in Baghdad assigning to him the governorship of all the lands of Transoxiana. The names of Isma'il and Nasr were mentioned with that of the caliph in the public prayers in Bukhara, a prerogative usually reserved for the caliph.

Isma'il had to subdue several robber bands in the oasis of

Bukhara, and then he repelled an invasion of the oasis by a certain Husain b. Tahir who probably was the same Husain mentioned above. Slowly his influence and power grew, but among other tasks he had to win over the nobles, headed by Abu Muhammad Bukhar Khudah. By a ruse he sent them to his brother in Samarqand, who took them into custody until Isma'il had further consolidated his position. Then they were returned to Bukhara, where Isma'il treated them well and enlisted their support.

A quarrel arose between the two brothers, probably over the amount of the taxes that Isma'il was to send every year to Samarqand. In any case, civil war did break out in 885, and at first Nasr seemed to be the victor since Isma'il was forced to evacuate Bukhara. We need not follow the course of the struggle, including a first reconciliation between the brothers, followed by further hostilities. In 888 Isma'il won a battle and captured his brother Nasr. The treatment of Nasr by Isma'il has been recorded in story to illustrate the generous character of the latter. The account goes that, when Isma'il met his older brother, he dismounted and showed obeisance toward Nasr, asking forgiveness for his errors and sins. Then he sent Nasr back to Samarqand, still the head of the Samanid family and ruler of Transoxiana. Nasr was much moved by this treatment and Isma'il gained a reputation for kindness and understanding which has come down in history. Nasr died in 892 after designating Isma'il his successor, and placing his own family under his protection.

The new ruler had to consolidate his realm, leading expeditions against would-be rebels or foes, in the course of which, he subdued the town of Taraz to the west of present-day

39

Bishkek, changing the chief church of the town into a mosque. Nestorian Christianity had spread among the Turks and even penetrated to China several centuries earlier than Isma'il's reign. Isma'il established his authority in Transoxiana by treaty with local dynasties or by installing as governors those members of the Samanid family who were his close supporters. For example, a younger brother, called Ishaq b. Ahmad, was made governor of Ferghana, instead of another brother who had supported Nasr against Isma'il. The kingdom needed unity, for a struggle with 'Amr, the brother and successor of Ya'qub b. Laith, was imminent.

In 898 'Amr was at the height of his power, and the Saffarids, as his dynasty is called, ruled most of Iran. The caliph in the same year was forced to appoint 'Amr as governor of Transoxiana, removing Isma'il who had been appointed in 893 after the death of Nasr. Although the patent of appointment from the caliph practically had no value, legally or more symbolically it meant that 'Amr had a right to rule the lands north of the Oxus River in place of the Samanids. It should be mentioned that 'Amr had captured and killed the amir of Khurasan, Rafi' b. Harthama, who had been appointed by the caliph as a successor of the Tahirids and as an opponent of the Saffarids. Several sources say that Rafi' was a friend of Isma'il, so there were a number of grounds for hostility between Samanids and Saffarids.

Unfortunately, our sources are contradictory about details of the war between Isma'il and 'Amr, but the final outcome was the capture of 'Amr in a battle near Balkh in the year 900. Many stories are told about the capture of 'Amr, that he alone was captured while his entire army fled without losing another man, killed or captured. Whether this is true, or that 'Amr was captured after severe fighting, as some of the sources say, cannot be verified. Suffice it to say that the capture of 'Amr must have made a great impression on contemporaries, since so much was written about the event. 'Amr was sent to Baghdad, where he was executed.

Isma'il received from the caliph the investiture for all of Khurasan, and he proceeded to add various other areas of Iran to his domain. This, in effect, was the end of the caliphal governors of Khurasan, for after the Samanids not even the pretence was maintained. There is no evidence that any of the Samanids paid regular taxes or tribute to the caliph, any more than did the Saffarids. From time to time, however, gifts or even token amounts of tribute were sent to Baghdad. The relations between the Samanids and the caliphs were much closer and better than between the Saffarids, or even the Tahirids, and Baghdad. When an heretical Shi'ite ruler from the Caspian province of Tabaristan tried to expand his power in 901, Isma'il sent an army against him, and after victory brought Tabaristan under Samanid rule. In Tabaristan the name of the reigning caliph was introduced into the Friday prayers by Isma'il, a practice maintained all over the Samanid domains. The following year Isma'il drove a rebel out of Rayy (present Tehran) and Qazvin at the request of the caliph. Although he then ruled the area, he sent from it a regular tribute to Baghdad.

An invasion of Turkish nomads over the northern frontiers of the Samanid domain led to a *jihad* or "holy war," proclaimed by Isma'il against the infidels. With the help of numerous Muslim volunteers, or "warriors of the faith,"

Samanid forces were able to repulse the invaders. This was in 904, and three years later Isma'il became sick and died in a suburb of Bukhara, which he loved. The so-called tomb of Isma'il, which is an important structure in the history of Islamic architecture and a tourist attraction of present-day Bukhara, probably dates from a slightly later period. The lovely mausoleum of light colored brick work, a good descendant of pre-Islamic Central Asian architecture and style, may be the family sepulchre of later Samanid princes, but still from Samanid times.

Isma'il was not only an empire builder but also, according to the sources, a man of great piety and a model of a prince. Nizam al-Mulk, the great minister of the Seljük Turks who ruled almost two centuries after Isma'il, wrote in high praise of this Samanid. He tells us that it was the custom of Isma'il to go alone on his horse to the central square of Bukhara, even when it was snowing and cold. He would remain there until the noon prayers. He justified this because of indigent or needy persons who might not otherwise have access to him or his court. Such people could always find him at the square and present a petition to him to right any wrongs done them.

Isma'il, according to Narshakhi, freed the people of the oasis from corvée and heavy payments to maintain the great walls. Isma'il claimed that while he lived, he was the wall of Bukhara. He not only made Bukhara the seat of government and built extensively in the city, but under him a kingdom was founded which recalled the ancient empires of Iran. Although much of his life was spent in organizing and administering the affairs of state, and in warfare, he yet found time to encourage learning and the arts.

Although the flowering of Bukhara occurred in the reign of his grandson, already under Isma'il scholars and literary men began to migrate to the city from other parts of the eastern Islamic world. In an anthology and biographical work on poets writing in Arabic, an author called Abu Mansur al-Tha'alibi, who lived in Nishapur, reveals the extent of the attraction of Bukhara for literary men. For example, in 907, the year of Isma'il's death, a poet called Abu Ja'far Muhammad b. al-'Abbas came from Baghdad to Bukhara because his father, the prime minister of the caliph, had fallen from grace. He came not only because it was a secure refuge far from Baghdad, but also because it was a flourishing center of power and culture. It would be tedious to list the names of poets, many of whom were also savants or employed in the bureaucracy of the Samanids, who came to Bukhara from Nishapur, Baghdad, Shash, and elsewhere. Such was the influx of scholars that Bukhara won the epithet "the dome of Islam in the east," equal to Baghdad, because it was such a great meeting place for distinguished men of letters. The security and prosperity established by Isma'il was the basis for the pre-eminent position of Bukhara.

We must not forget who Isma'il was and what he represented. He was of aristocratic lineage, descended from Saman, a local prince or *dihqan,* who himself was said to be descended from a Sasanian noble, Bahram Chobin. The traditions of the *dihqan* class must have permeated the society in which Isma'il moved, and the Samanids probably felt themselves protectors of this way of life. Certainly Islam had profoundly altered the pre-Islamic nature of the aristocratic society, but that society nonetheless survived even

43

though in a changed garb. The official written language of the Samanid bureaucracy under Isma'il was Arabic although Persian was the common spoken language of the towns-people, and in the countryside Sogdian dialects were spoken.

The bureaucracy was expanded under Isma'il, since Bukhara changed from a provincial city to the capital of an empire. The organization of the state is described in part by various authors such as Narshakhi, Nizam al-Mulk, al-Khwarazmi in his *Keys of the Sciences,* and others. We find information in later authors, too, for the Samanid organs of government served as models for the following dynasties of the Ghaznavids and Seljüks. Although the Samanid organization itself was patterned after the court in Baghdad, the spirit, or the archetypes, for both Baghdad and Bukhara, came from Sasanian Ctesiphon. This is specifically indicated by al-Khwarazmi, mentioned above, who gives Middle Persian names for several registers of the Samanid court. Since al-Khwarazmi himself was employed in that bureaucracy, his information is especially welcome. Firdosi in his epic describes the Sasanian court, but one feels that he also has the Samanids in mind, especially when he gives details about the rule of Chosroes Anushirvan, the great Sasanian monarch.

The sources then confirm the natural surmise that the Samanids combined in their own court Islam and Sasanian Iran. At the head of the government stood the *vezir,* the prime minister. The word *vezir* is a fascinating example of the frequent confusion between Arabic and Persian, with a voluminous literature in defense of one or the other etymology of the word. The word is Iranian, just as is the word *divan,* meaning "place of archives," but to many such words

44

the Arabs gave Arabic forms and even origins. A good knowledge of Arabic was, of course, essential for the scribes and functionaries of state, and there is no evidence of conflict over language in the *divans,* as the bureaus of state were known. This again is in harmony with the traditional attitude of the scribes from ancient times. Writing was a profession plied by a jealous class or caste, and letters and other writings were not intended to represent the speech of the common man.

Under Isma'il, we hear of a minister called Abu'l-Fadl al-Bal'ami and a chief scribe named Abu Bakr b. Hamid. Since the ruler himself was such a strong figure, his ministers do not appear in the limelight in the sources. They, however, probably built the system of bureaus more than did Isma'il. Under the caliphs, the government of the provinces was divided between the *amir,* or governor, and the *'amil,* or tax collector. The Samanids, copying Baghdad, applied the provincial principle to their districts, so that the Samanid domains mirrored the caliphate. Even as the various bureaus of the chancery were separated from the court in Baghdad, so there were two organs of rule in Bukhara. Just as the caliph had his guard of slaves and pages, so did Isma'il at his court. And just as Turkish slaves came to dominate the caliph's guard in Baghdad, so did the Turks outnumber others at the Samanid court, especially following the reign of Isma'il. Various offices and titles are found in the court of the Samanids, some of them military and others domestic. The captain of the royal guard was probably the top official of the court military establishment, and the *wakil,* or "manager," of internal court affairs, probably of the domestic part of the court. To the court came savants, poets, and others seeking remuneration from the *amir* or from one of his favorites. The importance of the court grew under later Samanid rulers, to the detriment of the bureaucracy or civil service.

The bureaucracy was headed by the *vezir,* and there were a number of offices or bureaus under him. Narshakhi enumerates ten *divans* at Bukhara, all of them physically located near the citadel where the ruler resided. One *divan* functioned as the treasury or bureau of taxes, the importance of which is obvious. Another office is probably best described as that of the archives and documents, and a third was devoted to army affairs. The office of the post not only transmitted letters but also was an information or espionage center. The *divan* of the private property of the ruler may have been under the direction of the *wakil,* for much of the wealth of the ruler was in land. Still another bureau was concerned with police functions, internal order, such as the control of weights and measures, and the like. For a time there seems to have been an important bureau of foundations, or *awqaf,* as they were called, a bureau of great importance even in some contemporary Islamic states. The judicial department was a government within a government, since the religious leaders at times championed private individuals against the state in lawsuits, all of which were judged in religious courts by religious judges, called *qadi* in Arabic.

The author of a book of biographies, al-Sam'ani, tells us that the chief religious figure at the court of Isma'il was called *al-ustadh,* "master," and his influence far exceeded religious affairs. Religious leaders among the populace had

46

taken the lead in inviting Isma'il to Bukhara, and some time later, after the fall of the Samanids, the religious chiefs of the Hanafite school of law of the family of Burhan, called *sadrs,* held the political as well as the spiritual power in Bukhara. The influence which the religious leaders had over the masses in medieval Bukhara can be compared with that of their counterparts, the *mujtahids* in Shi'ite Iran today.

The piety of Isma'il and the favor he bestowed on the re-ligious savants in his kingdom established a strong relation-ship between the Samanid rulers and their subjects. This accounts in some measure for the praise and the high esteem held for the dynasty by Persian writers, whether historians or poets. It should be mentioned, of course, that other than poets, most authors in medieval Islamic times were religious judges or leaders, hence they are naturally somewhat parti-san. In several books, a certain Khwaja Imam Abu Hafs, who died about 877, is credited with establishing the supremacy of the Hanafite law school in Bukhara and of attracting to the city distinguished doctors of jurisprudence. Bukhara's role under the Samanids as a center of Hanafite law may have originated with Abu Hafs.

What was established at the capital of Bukhara became the model for the provincial centers, and we find a parallel development on a smaller scale outside of the royal court. Since the Samanids represented the conservative traditions of the aristocracy, and the *status quo* as opposed to the somewhat revolutionary government of the Saffarids, the provincial administration was not overhauled or unified. The rule of local lords or princes was maintained within the Samanid empire, if it may be so called. The rulers of various parts of the Samanid domains are called margraves or "frontier lords" in a tenth-century Persian geography called the *Regions of the World*.

So the state established by Isma'il was by no means uniform, since local princes existed as well as governors sent by the court of Bukhara, but since the interests of the *dihqan* class were not injured, but rather fostered, by the loose Samanid system of rule, they supported the Samanids and the kingdom lasted for more than a century.

Isma'il himself was not remiss in acquiring land for his family, and Narshakhi tells us that the *amir* bought the extensive lands of a descendant of the Bukhar Khudahs and added them to his own holdings. He also acquired the estates on a plain near the citadel of Bukhara called Juy-i Muliyan, which were described by poets as a part of paradise. Here Isma'il erected villas and gardens and he gave pieces of property in those vast estates to his favorites as well as to members of his family. The donations of land were probably early examples of the feudal system of granting land for military service called *iqta'*, which became so widespread under the later Seljüks. It is of interest to note that certain lands in Bukhara remained in the hands of descendants of the Samanids down almost to our own day.

Narshakhi gives an account of the death of Isma'il which may be of interest. He says that moisture aggravated his sickness. "Doctors said that the atmosphere of Juy-i Muliyan was wet, so he was carried to the village of Zarman, which was his private property. They said that this air would be better for him. The *amir* liked that village and always went there for hunting. A garden had been made for him. He

48

was sick there for some time until he died in a certain garden under a large tree in 907. His corpse was carried to Bukhara and buried and his tomb became a place of pilgrimage for the people of the city. May God show mercy on him, for in his time Bukhara became the seat of government. After him all the *amirs* of the house of Saman held court in Bukhara. None of the *amirs* of Khurasan before him had lived in Bukhara. He considered his residence in Bukhara as fortunate, and he did not find satisfaction in any district save Bukhara. Wherever he was he used to say that his city, Bukhara, had such and such. After his death his son took his place, and Isma'il was surnamed the late *amir.*"

· 4 ·
the Dome of Islam

That Bukhara is a mine of knowledge;
So whoever possesses wisdom is a Bukharan.
                    MAWLANA JALAL AL-DIN RUMI

AFTER THE DEATH OF ISMA'IL, his son Ahmad mounted the
throne. Ahmad was named after his grandfather, an ancient
Indo-European custom, and it seems was the governor of
Khurasan at the time of his father's death. One of his first
tasks was to go to Samarqand, where he arrested his uncle
Ishaq, probably the eldest prominent Samanid alive. Ishaq
was brought to Bukhara and imprisoned, so the control of
the family passed into Ahmad's hands. Ahmad then conquered the province of Seistan, which had been granted to
his father by the caliph and reconfirmed after Ahmad's accession. The province at that time was occupied by the
descendants of Ya'qub b. Laith, and only after much fighting and several revolts did Seistan acknowledge Samanid
supremacy.

We have said that the official written language of the
bureaucracy at Bukhara was Arabic, but a curious remark by
Hamdallah Qazvini, a historian of the fourteenth century,
that *amir* Ahmad changed the proclamations and decrees
from Persian to Arabic, needs to be explained. This statement, I believe, is interesting evidence for the bilingualism
of the court. The usual spoken language was Persian, while

50

the written language was Arabic. In addresses to the people, decrees were read from an Arabic text but put into Persian. Ahmad, who was very pious like his father, and who was attracted to Arabic-speaking savants who had come to Bukhara, evidently decided that the decrees written in Arabic should be proclaimed in Arabic too. If people were unable or unwilling to learn Arabic, then so much the worse for them. This experiment, along with other reasons, led to opposition to the *amir*, with the result that he was murdered in his tent, during a trip, by his own slaves. This happened in 914.

The new ruler, Nasr, son of Ahmad, was only eight years old when his father was killed; but he was fortunate in having a remarkable man as prime minister, Abu 'Abdallah Muhammad b. Ahmad Jaihani. We shall speak of Jaihani below in connection with the cultural flowering in Bukhara.

Ahmad's uncle Ishaq had been released from prison in 911 and sent to govern Samarqand, while in the following year Mansur, one son of Ishaq, had been named as governor in Nishapur. With the death of Ahmad, both revolted and the throne of Nasr seemed very insecure. The army of Nasr, however, proved equal to the demands on it and Ishaq was defeated and brought to Bukhara. Mansur died in Nishapur but another son, Ilyas, fled to Ferghana and raised a revolt which lasted until 922, when it was suppressed and the successful general Muhammad b. Asad, another Samanid prince, was installed as governor of Ferghana. Ilyas continued to intrigue but was eventually pardoned and returned to Bukhara. Troubles and uprisings, however, continued to plague the kingdom of the Samanids, and much warfare was necessary in Seistan and western Iran to maintain Samanid rule on the plateau of Iran.

More serious were internal troubles, primarily religious. Sectarian movements had flourished in the eastern part of the caliphate since the time of the Umayyads, and partisans of the house of 'Ali, the Shi'ites, were to be found everywhere. Certainly Iran was neither the original home nor even the most receptive territory for Shi'ite ideas, as has been asserted by some scholars. Although Shi'ite missionaries were especially successful in the Caspian provinces of Iran and in Seistan, Sunni orthodoxy was dominant elsewhere, even though pockets of Shi'ites existed in towns such as Qum. We cannot go into the branches of the Shi'ites which developed during the early 'Abbasid caliphate. Suffice it to say that a rebirth of Shi'ite activity occurred in the second half of the ninth century, culminating in the establishment of a new counter caliphate in North Africa in 909. These Shi'ites, called the Fatimids, followed a line of succession different from other Shi'ites, who supported the claims of twelve *imams,* or leaders, descended in strict order of father to son from the caliph 'Ali, son-in-law of the prophet Muhammad. The Fatimids followed another line of *imams* after the seventh *imam* Isma'il. Hence they were called Isma'ilis, or also "Seveners."

Isma'ili missionaries had appeared in western Iran, in the vicinity of Rayy near modern Tehran, shortly before the year 900. Little is known of their early activities, but we may surmise that they won adherents primarily among other Shi'ites. Shortly after 900, the first leader of the missionary work *(da'wa)* in Khurasan, a certain Abu 'Abdallah al-

52

Khadim, is mentioned by several sources. He resided in Nishapur but sent lieutenants to various cities of Khurasan and Transoxiana. It is possible that the failure of the Isma'ili missionaries to convert many of the common people in western Iran led to a change of tactics in the east. The establishment of the Fatimid caliphate too may have brought about a change in policy. For the Isma'ili missionaries in Khurasan concentrated on converting the upper classes and the government bureaucracy. The Isma'ilis were lucky in the conversion of an important Samanid general called al-Husain al-Marwazi sometime during the reign of Ahmad b. Isma'il. At the death of the *amir* Ahmad b. Isma'il, al-Marwazi was one of the many rebels against the central authority, but in 918 he was defeated and captured near his native city of Merv al-Rud and brought to Bukhara. After a time in prison, al-Marwazi was released and became active at the court of Nasr b. Ahmad. While he was at the court, sometime between 920 and 925, he became chief of the Isma'ili *da'wa* in Khurasan. Thus the Isma'ilis had attained a high position at court through him in a relatively short period.

It was the successor of al-Marwazi who had the most success in Isma'ili conversions. He came from a city in Transoxiana called Nakhshab or Nasaf, hence his name Muhammad b. Ahmad al-Nakhshabi. He was not only an ardent missionary but also a learned author, and one of the leading figures in the formation of Isma'ili philosophical doctrines. Although he did work among the people, he aimed higher, and the brilliant court of Nasr b. Ahmad was a receptive ground for philosophical discussions as well as for non-conformity. Even Nizam al-Mulk, prime minister of the Seljüks, admitted that Nakhshabi was one of the group of brilliant savants assembled in Bukhara by the *amir* Nasr.

It is impossible to go into Isma'ili doctrines in detail here, but a few words about them are necessary. Essentially, Persian Isma'ilism was a form of Islamic Neoplatonism or Gnosticism, with great emphasis on allegory and a hidden interpretation of most passages of the Quran. Since the Isma'ilis believed in a secret *(batin)* meaning as well as the common meaning of religious injunctions, they have been called Batinis in many sources. Only the Isma'ili *imam* or his missionaries could comprehend and teach the hidden meanings of the prophet's revelations.

Unfortunately, none of the writings of Nakhshabi have survived, and we only have very brief extracts, probably rewritten, of what may have been his major work, the *Mahsul,* preserved in later Isma'ili books. They are not sufficient to give a picture of the ideas of Nakhshabi, but we may infer that most of the Isma'ili doctrines, such as the universal soul and universal reason under God, expectation of the messiah, and others, were expounded in Nakhshabi's teachings and writings. Since Nakhshabi came to the sophisticated court of Bukhara, we may further assume that his philosophical expositions were more significant than his religious preaching, more directed to the common folk. In any case, he won over to the Isma'ili cause some of the leading figures of the court such as the *amir*'s private secretary, Abu Mansur Chaghani, the inspector of the army, the chamberlain, and others. Eventually, he succeeded in converting the *amir* Nasr himself.

Some Isma'ili teachings must have appeared as dualistic

54

to orthodox Muslims, hence as outright infidelity, or apostasy, which was worse in Islam. Such ideas of an external, revealed law and an internal, secret law to be expounded by the *imam,* however, were probably less offensive than the common belief that the Isma'ili leaders, by virtue of their gnosis or esoteric knowledge, were allowed to cast off all rites and beliefs. Whatever the reality in accusations, for example, that the Isma'ilis had a hierarchy of grades like the hated Manichaeans, there is no question that the Isma'ilis aroused violent opposition wherever they went. So Nasr's conversion must have greatly upset the orthodox Sunni leaders in the city of Bukhara.

It is difficult to believe that *amir* Nasr acknowledged allegiance to the Fatimid caliph in Africa, as some sources indicate, for on the coins struck by Nasr we find the names of 'Abbasid caliphs. It would seem that a real conversion, if it did take place, was a personal matter and did not intrude into public policy. Unless, of course, Nasr had certain political ends in view by supporting the Isma'ilis, but the Fatimids were far away, and we do not know any motives for an alliance. One reason for the public dislike of non-Sunnis was the capture of Mecca by Shi'ite sectarians called Qarmatians, co-religionists of the Fatimids, in 930. The sack of the city, with great destruction and slaughter, spread dismay throughout the Islamic world, including the Samanid domains.

Nizam al-Mulk tells us that the officers of the Samanid army plotted to assassinate Nasr and name the commander-in-chief of the army the new ruler. In a detailed story, he tells how the commander organized a banquet to gather his officers for the uprising, but Nuh, the son of Nasr, learned of the preparations and acted swiftly, decapitating the commander. He persuaded his father to abdicate, and thus he stopped a revolt. This occurred in the year of 332 of the Hegira, or 943 A.D., a black event for the Isma'ilis. Nuh shortly ordered Nakhshabi executed, and all of the Isma'ilis in Samanid domains who could be found were similarly treated. This catastrophe ended Isma'ili hopes in Khurasan and Transoxiana, and they never regained a comparable position of importance in Bukhara or anywhere north of the Oxus River. Sunni Islam reigned supreme ever afterwards.

It was during the reign of Nasr that Bukhara rose to new eminence as a center of culture and learning. More than Nasr himself, his two *vezirs,* or prime ministers, were the main patrons of the savants and literary men. The first was Abu 'Abdallah Muhammad b. Ahmad al-Jaihani, who held office from 914 to 922 and again from 938 to 941. He is famous as the author of a geography, which has not survived, but which provided information about the non-Islamic lands of the north and east to later geographers. Jaihani was also known as a highly cultured person, interested in astronomy and the sciences as well as in the arts, and one author, Gardizi, says he wrote many books about various sciences. His own inquiring mind and his investigations, as well as his patronage of others, gave him fame in the Islamic world during his lifetime. He subsidized one of the earliest and most competent of the geographers, Abu Zaid al-Balkhi, but the latter refused to leave his native city of Balkh to come to Bukhara at the invitation of the *vezir.*

It was at the end of Jaihani's term of office that the embassy of the caliph al-Muqtadir to the king of the Bulghars on the Volga River passed through Bukhara. Ibn Fadlan, the ambassador, wrote an account of his journey in which he speaks well of the *vezir* and says Jaihani was known throughout Khurasan as *al-shaikh al-'amid* "the supporting chief," evidence of the use of honorifics in the Samanid domains. Jaihani was evidently very interested in Ibn Fadlan's mission, as he was in other travelers. Ibn Fadlan, incidentally, does not call Jaihani *vezir* but rather scribe *(katib)*, the former term probably being reserved for the prime minister of the caliph, at least in Ibn Fadlan's mind.

Jaihani was suspected of Shi'ite inclinations, or even of Manichaean dualist sentiments, but it is not known if his removal from office was linked with such accusations. His successor was Abu'l Fadl al-Bal'ami, who has been mentioned in the pages devoted to Isma'il, founder of the Samanid dynasty. Bal'ami was probably an official in the bureaucracy under Isma'il, but hardly the prime minister, as some sources have claimed. He held the post of *vezir* for over fifteen years, from about 922 to 938, after which he lived only two more years. Bal'ami continued what might be called the enlightened or liberal policy of his predecessor. He also showed his diplomatic ability on one occasion, about 930, when a revolt broke out in Bukhara during the absence of the *amir* in Nishapur. The rebels, including three brothers of Nasr, seized the city and seemed in control of affairs. The *vezir,* by stirring up the rebels against each other, was able to quell the revolt with a minimum of bloodshed.

It is the cultural, social and economic life of Bukhara during the reign of Nasr, however, which is of prime interest for us. Of course, Baghdad continued to be the cultural center of the Islamic world, and the ninth century saw the great work of al-Ash'ari in establishing the theological basis of Sunni orthodoxy, the medical and scientific writings of Sinan b. Thabit b. Qurra, and the great history of Tabari. All of the aforementioned lived in Baghdad, but the provincial centers reflected the splendor of the capital, and none more than Bukhara. We have already mentioned poets and savants employed in the Samanid bureaucracy, and it would seem that employment by the government was the chief means of patronage for men of letters. That they were welcomed into the bureaucracy indicates the interest of the government, from the *amir* down, in cultural and scientific pursuits.

The cultural flowering, of course, was not restricted to the court. Ibn Sina, called Avicenna in the Latin West, spent his childhood in Bukhara at the end of Samanid rule, but the glimpses of the capital which we gain from his works also applied to the earlier period. Ibn Sina says that the book bazaar in Bukhara was unequalled, and in one of the shops he found a manuscript work of the philosopher al-Farabi, which helped him to understand better the teachings of Aristotle. Most probably, as even today in the Orient, the proprietors of the book stalls were learned men, and the shops were forums and social centers where poets, philosophers, doctors, astronomers, and others gathered to discuss affairs. Astronomy and astrology were well cultivated not only because of widespread belief in astrology, but also because of the need to determine correctly the times of prayer,

58

the beginning and end of religious holidays, and the concordance between solar and lunar years.

Ibn Sina lived and studied in Bukhara under the *amir* Nuh b. Mansur (976–97) but the royal library which he describes was assembled in earlier reigns. Ibn Sina says the royal library was composed of a number of rooms, each room being reserved for manuscripts of a certain art or specialty; for example, one room contained books in Islamic law; another was reserved for poetry. The manuscripts were kept in chests, but the amount of labor and time spent on copying books in Bukhara must have been enormous. Paper was relatively new and there cannot have been a great abundance of it, even though it was certainly cheaper than parchment.

Perhaps more than anything else which gave Bukhara fame was the sheer number of savants gathered there. An oft-quoted passage in the anthology of Abu Mansur al-Tha'alibi, mentioned above, deserves to be repeated since it reveals the contemporary feeling. "Bukhara was under Samanid rule, the focus of splendor, the shrine of empire, the meeting place of the most unique intellects of the age, the horizon of the literary stars of the world, and the fair of the greatest scholars of the period. Abu Ja'far al-Musavi related, 'my father Abu'l-Hasan received an invitation to Bukhara in the days of the *amir*-i Sa'id [Nasr], and there were gathered together the most remarkable of its men of letters, such as [list of names] ... And my father said to me, "O my son, this is a notable and memorable day; make it an epoch as regards the assembling of the standards of talent and the most incomparable scholars of the age, and remember it, when I am gone, amongst the great occasions of the age and the notable moments of thy life. For I scarcely think that in the lapse of the years thou wilt see the like of these met together." And so it was, for never again was my eye brightened with the sight of such a gathering.' "

The pride of the court was poetry and much has been written about the poetry of the Samanid age. It is essential, I believe, to remember that the literature, and especially poetry, under the Samanids was one literature in two languages, Arabic and Persian. Although the geographers assure us that Sogdian was also spoken at Bukhara in this period, it was surely a dying tongue of the peasants. It should be emphasized again that Arabic was employed not only in prayers and sermons, but also in all writings on religious subjects, juridical literature, science, and philosophy. We have noted that the bureaucratic writings were in Arabic and a clerk had to know Arabic to qualify for a position. The influx of scholars and poets to Bukhara which began under Isma'il continued, but many savants from Transoxiana went to Baghdad. There was a Sogdian colony in Baghdad, and Samarra, the temporary 'Abbasid capital for a time, was almost a Central Asian city. We cannot discuss the poets from Transoxiana who lived in Baghdad and who wrote in Arabic, such as Ibn Quhi, al-Khuraimi, Khalifa al-Akhmai, and others. Likewise, the poets from various parts of the caliphate who came to Bukhara, writing in Arabic, fill many pages in the anthology of al-Tha'alibi. More interesting are those poets in Bukhara who composed poems both in Arabic and in Persian, and those who translated Persian poetry into Arabic, or vice versa.

To discuss first the translators, it is interesting that the translations from Persian to Arabic were not from ancient or non-Islamic Persian sources, but from contemporary poets. It is possible, as has been claimed, that the anti-Arab movement, called the *Shuʻubiyya,* was responsible for many of such translations, since the translations into Arabic demonstrated the importance of Persian to a wide audience throughout the caliphate. However, since the Persian and Arabic poetry of the bilingual poets is not only the same in content, but also in form, the *Shuʻubiyya* was not the dominant reason for the translations. Since the poets were all Muslims, and relatively few non-Muslim traits are revealed in the vast bulk of the poetry, it would seem more likely that the poets originally composed in their native Persian tongue, but then to show their skill, and perhaps also to reach an audience in the Arabic-speaking part of the caliphate, they made translations into Arabic. The main sources for the translations in this period, other than the anthology of al-Thaʻalibi, are a book called *Lubab,* by Muhammad ʻAufi, written in the twelfth century, and several tracts on translation.

Many Arabic prose works were translated into Persian because, as one translator said, "people were too lazy to learn Arabic." Most of these translations were made under the later Samanids, such as the Persian translation of Tabari's *Tafsir,* or commentary on the Quran, and the same author's history. Both translations were ordered by the son of al-Balʻami, *vezir* of the *amir* Mansur b. Nuh (961–76). The reasons for such translations are not difficult to imagine, but poetry was another matter, and it is significant that older, classical Arabic poems, rather than contemporary Arabic poetry, were translated into Persian. Since Arabic was the *lingua franca* of the Islamic world and had a large literature, to what other literary sources could any educated Muslim turn for information? Even the reported Persian translation of the ancient fables of Kalila and Dimna by Rudaki was probably based on the Arabic text of Ibn al-Muqaffa', who had translated it from Pahlavi, which in turn was translated from Sanskrit. Under the Samanids, poems of early Islamic Arab poets such as Ibn al-Rumi and Farazdak were translated into Persian, but not Arabic poetry of the ninth or tenth centuries. Local poets could write their own poems in Arabic or Persian, and their Arabic poems are in no way distinguishable from Arabic poems by native Arabs.

There is no question that the enriching of the Persian language by Arabic words, and the change from simple syllabic poetry of Middle Iranian to the elaborate formal poetry based on the Arabic system of long and short syllables, gave New Persian a tremendous catalyst for the creation of literature. New Persian poetry of the Samanid period is basically Islamic and mostly copied from Arabic poetry, which in turn derived its rules of versification from Greek. Great controversy has arisen over the term *Dari* used in many sources to describe the Persian language of this period. Some scholars have gone so far as to claim that it was really a different language, perhaps a descendant of Parthian or Sogdian. It seems, however, that *Dari*, presumably the "court" language, was really a simple style of New Persian free from Arabic words, whereas the term *Farsi* in this period was a designation of the style of the New Persian language which was greatly mixed with Arabic words and was ornate rather than simple. This latter style became so predominant that *Dari* went out of use. An interesting indication of this was a book of Sindbad the sage translated into *Dari* by order of Nuh b. Nasr in 950, but some two hundred years later "translated" from *Dari* into Persian because the simple *Dari* text was archaic and "stood on the path of forgetfulness," hence needed to be adorned by the style of the time.

Some scholars have thought that the Middle Iranian tongue, the official language of the Sasanian Empire called Pahlavi, was read and even written by poets such as Rudaki. This is extremely unlikely, and even the existence of Zoroastrian *mobads,* or priests, in Bukhara who could read Pahlavi is open to question. The difficult Pahlavi script had been always restricted in use, mainly to the religious hierarchy of the Zoroastrian church, and it is difficult to believe that Pahlavi had many devotees in Samanid Bukhara. It is claimed that the *Dari* translation of the book of Sindbad, mentioned above, was made from Pahlavi and not from Arabic. Given the intellectual curiosity of the court circles at Bukhara, this is by no means improbable, but if so it was a curiosity and not at all usual.

The jewel of the court of Nasr was Abu 'Abdallah Ja'far b. Muhammad Rudaki, probably from a village called Rudak, present Panj Rud, east of Samarqand. The dates of his life are not known, but he was advanced in years during the reign of Nasr and died shortly before Nuh b. Nasr ascended the throne. Rudaki began his career as a traditional minstrel, composing and singing poems to the people of his native village. Unfortunately, we do not know when he came to Bukhara, or indeed any details of his life, but he flourished at the court of Nasr, who richly rewarded Rudaki for his poems. At the end of his life, however, it seems he had to leave the court in disgrace, possibly because of his sympathy for Nakhshabi and his heretical views. He has been described as a poet blind from birth, but the discovery of his tomb and skeleton in his native village enabled Soviet scientists to show that he died at a ripe old age, at that time possibly blind, but not from birth.

Rudaki was considered the greatest of the early Persian poets, and later poets of the eleventh and twelfth centuries emulated his style. In fact his poems are preserved only in the notices, anthologies, or dictionaries of later authors. Rudaki was a master of the panegyric or *qasida,* an ode in praise of one's patron. But Rudaki was not just a paid praiser of the *amir;* many different meters are used by him, and the motifs of the cup and wine and others, so common in later poetry, also are found in Rudaki's fragments. Their meaning and significance in Rudaki's poems, however, is simple and straightforward, not with the involved mystical implications of later Sufi poetry. Rudaki is generally known as a lyric poet, and the question whether the later widespread form of poetry known as the *ghazal* was used by Rudaki has been long debated. As usual, the answer to this question depends on definitions. If one means by *ghazal* a wide term relating to the motif of love of a man for a woman, then it certainly exists in Rudaki's compositions. If, more narrowly, one is concerned with the technical development of the *ghazal,* as exemplified by the masterpieces of a Hafiz, then the *ghazal* did not yet exist in Rudaki's time. Certainly the incipient forms of later Persian poetry are to be found in the

64

Samanid period, and the simplicity of some of the early
poetry can be deceiving, while at the same time delightful
in comparison with the highly stylized productions of later
times.

To return to Rudaki, he was the *primus inter pares* of the
Samanid poets. One talented student of Rudaki called Abu'l
Hasan Shahid Balkhi died before his master did and is la-
mented in a poem by Rudaki. Rudaki's skill in rousing the
emotions is well illustrated by the popular story of how he, at
the instigation of homesick army officers, persuaded the *amir*
Nasr to return from the vicinity of Herat to Bukhara after
the *amir* had been absent a long time. He composed a
famous verse which began, "the Juy-i Muliyan we call to
mind; / We long for those dear friends left behind." The
poem includes the lines at the beginning of chapter three,
and such was the effect of the poem on the *amir* that he
mounted his horse and set off for Bukhara without his riding
boots. The army is said to have paid Rudaki handsomely
for his poem. It is noteworthy that a later compiler of poems
called Daulatshah remarked it was astonishing that such
simple verses could move a ruler, since they were lacking
in embellishment and artifices. He continued that if anyone
made such a poem in his time (1487) it would receive the
ridicule of everyone. He concludes that the success of this
simple poem was probably based on the fact that Rudaki
sang it to the accompaniment of a musical instrument. So
had Persian poetry developed long after Rudaki!

If one reads the poetry of Rudaki, he is struck by the
pessimism and references to shortness of life and the sadness
of man's fate. But this is paralleled with a joy of life and

CENTRAL ASIA AND KHURASAN
IN THE TENTH CENTURY

66

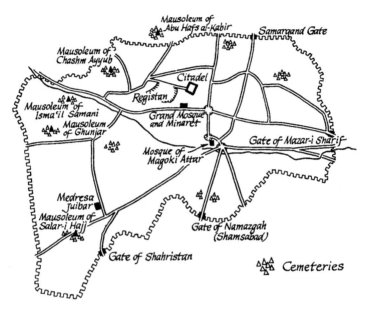

BUKHARA IN THE TENTH AND ELEVENTH CENTURIES
(After O. A. Sukhareva, *K Istorii Gorodov Bukharskogo
Khanstva* [Tashkent, 1958])

sympathy which permeate good Persian poetry throughout
the ages. Even this early poetry is subtle in the variety of
images and meanings which may be evoked from it. In
regard to themes, the allusions to Zoroaster and an apparent
rejection of Islam by several of the Samanid poets should
not be taken as evidence that they were non-Muslims, but
rather that formal religion weighed lightly on the external
lives of these humanists. Zoroaster was really a symbol of
a kind of leader in a garden of Eden for them.

It would be tedious to list the names of poets who had the
ethnic appellation Bukhari, or those who were known to
have lived in Bukhara under the Samanids. The relations
between the sophisticated court poets and the ruder minstrels who composed and even sang for the people are not
revealed by our sources. Incidentally, the Arab practice of
a reciter, or *rawi,* accompanying the poet, was also found
in the domains of Iranian languages. One may conjecture
that the later ill feeling between the court poets and their
commoner minstrel brethren also existed in early times,
although the sentiments and connections, if any, between
poets and singers are not clear. Rudaki's life spanned both
of these arts or crafts, and this must have been true of others.
The language of the minstrel was popular, with words not
used by court poets who composed *qasidas* in a high style.
Such a division between popular oral and stylized written
literature has existed elsewhere and for a long time in the
Orient.

Other literature existed, even though overshadowed by
poetry. Although the vast majority of writings in prose were
in Arabic, we hear of a Persian book on the Isma'ili esoteric
interpretation of the Quran by a missionary in the time of
Nasr. This is not unexpected, since missionary work was
primarily directed to the people, more of whom would understand Persian than Arabic. A history of Bukhara in Arabic
was written under Nasr, and later the history of Narshakhi,
who died in 959, also in Arabic.

Muslims, like the ancient Greeks, were interested in theories of science and mathematics but not much in their appli-
cations. We have mentioned their interest in astronomy and

astrology, but how was knowledge transmitted in this age? Later we learn of colleges, such as the famous Nizamiyya in Baghdad, where Islamic jurisprudence, philosophy, and the sciences were systematically taught. There existed at least some kind of a curriculum, but in the Samanid period there is no evidence of a school system. Rather knowledge was transmitted on a master-to-apprentice basis, and students would gather about a savant because of his renown in a certain field or endeavor. Book shops and salon gatherings have been mentioned as centers of learning. In contemporary Europe, the torch of learning was feebly maintained by a few monasteries, the like of which did not exist in the Muslim world.

In some practical affairs the inhabitants of the Samanid domains were advanced for their time. One of these areas was irrigation and the distribution of water, since water was a matter of life or death. Bukhara's neighboring city, Samarqand, was noted for its system of lead pipes for the distribution of water, and we may presume that Bukhara was not far behind. The network of canals in the oasis of Bukhara, combined with the intricate riparian rights of the cultivators made of irrigation a subject of study and constant concern for all of the inhabitants of the oasis. The famous underground water conduits, later called *kariz,* were in operation in this period, although they were not needed as much in the Bukharan oasis as elsewhere in Central Asia or Iran.

Rice was raised in irrigated areas of the oasis, but wheat and other cereals as well as various kinds of cotton were also important products. It is clear that the kind of agriculture practiced in the oasis of Bukhara inspired a feudal society, but with a tendency towards centralization. The latter was necessary to maintain the common struggle against the sands of the desert, and we hear of great gangs of peasants working on irrigation projects or on wall building at forced labor. From literary sources and archaeology it is clear that the aristocracy was numerous, occupying many villas and castles throughout the oasis. Another interesting feature of land ownership gleaned from the literary sources was a wide-spread absentee ownership of land. Officials of the caliph, as well as the commander of the faithful himself, owned plots of land in Khurasan and Central Asia, while members of the upper classes in the Samanid domains sometimes owned houses in Baghdad or estates elsewhere in Iraq.

Technology was not greatly advanced over previous centuries, and papermaking, which Chinese prisoners are supposed to have taught their captors in Samarqand after 751, is the only outstanding new discovery with important consequences. Samarqand continued to be a center of paper-making in Samanid times. Oil was extracted from the ground in the Ferghana valley, although we have no details on methods employed. One important use of oil seems to have been in warfare. In sieges of towns, special clay pipes were filled with oil and hurled inside the walls by catapults, where-upon they burst into flames. It is possible that the use of such devices spread to Europe via the nomads of South Russia, although again details are lacking.

The trading activities of the people of Transoxiana, which have been mentioned, continued under the Samanids, and if anything they expanded, especially with eastern Europe. Caravans sometimes were almost the size of small armies.

The caravan with the embassy of Ibn Fadlan to the king of
the Bulghars on the upper Volga River was composed of
five thousand men and three thousand horses and camels,
but this was unusual. Most of the wares sent to eastern
Europe were luxury objects, such as the best kind of silk
and cotton goods, silver and copper bowls and plates, weapons, jewelry, and the like. From eastern Europe came furs,
amber, honey, sheep skins, and similar raw materials. The
great silk route to China also flourished under the Samanids,
and this time China was the sender of such luxuries as
pottery and spices and raw materials to the domain of the
Samanids. The Chinese, in turn, imported horses and,
among other articles, glass, for which Samarqand and other
centers in Transoxiana were famous.

   The Khwarazmians played the leading role in trade with
eastern Europe, as the Sogdians did with China. We have
evidence of Khwarazmian merchants in considerable numbers in the kingdom of the Khazars in south Russia and
among the Bulghars of the Volga. Such was their influence
that the Russians came to use Busurman, the Khwarazmian
pronunciation of the word Muslim or Musulman, for all
Central Asians. This term persisted in Russia long after the
Mongol conquest and was reported by European travelers to
Mongolia in the thirteenth century. Furthermore, the Caspian Sea was called the sea of Khvalis or Khwarazmians in
Old Russian chronicles. It is interesting to note that some
Christians in Khwarazm were Orthodox, under the metro-
politan of the Crimea, a further evidence of close contacts
with Russia. Khwarazm was primarily an entrepôt for the
exchange of goods. A twelfth-century geographer called

Yaqut tells of a merchant in his time who had a large ware-house in Khwarazm, another one in the city Bulghar (near the later Kazan) on the Volga, and a third in Gujarat in India. Thus spices, so necessary for meat in the days before refrigeration, were brought to eastern Europe.

The large volume of trade with eastern Europe is well attested by the quantities of Samanid silver coins found in Russia, Poland, and Scandinavia. The tenth century was a period of Viking expansion, so far-flung contacts were not unusual. Hoards of Samanid coins, as well as fewer "Bukhar Khudah" coins, have been found, many of them broken in half, so it would seem that the silver coins were used as currency as well as for pure exchange in eastern Europe. Silver always has been the currency of the steppes, and merchants from Samanid domains found that the nomads of Central Asia and south Russia would willingly accept their coins. But the coins had to be of good silver, since we find very few debased silver coins in the Scandinavian or Russian hoards. In China and in eastern Turkistan, on the contrary, no hoards of Samanid coins have been found, indicating, as the sources also report, that the Chinese did not accept silver coins but bartered goods with the caravans from the west. The caravans were composed not only of merchants, servants, and guards, but also of craftsmen and missionaries, indeed miniature towns on the move. And they brought their customs and culture with them. Just as the Sogdian merchants brought Iranian culture to the Far East, so did the Khwarazmians to eastern Europe, and in both instances the routes were dotted with caravansarais.

About every eighteen to twenty miles, the normal daily

distance traversed by a caravan, buildings were erected to facilitate the voyages of merchants. Some caravansarais have survived down to the present and are solid structures of stone, or of logs in eastern Russia. Others developed into towns or villages, but they generally followed a line of water holes or sites of easy defense. For the caravans were accompanied by guards, since the routes were frequently infested with bandits and nomadic tribes.

Much of the population of Central Asia and what is today Afghanistan went about their daily tasks with weapons. Consequently it was easy for a feudal lord to call his peasants together as an armed band, and there were many such lords in eastern Iran. Perhaps it would be better to call them *dihqans,* or country squires, because great feudal lords really came into their own only in the later Seljük period, when military leaders, as a reward for service to the ruler, were given large appanages or *'iqta's,* similar to the fiefs in western Europe.

The organization of caravans, *sarais,* guards, and the rest, was a complicated affair, so joint companies were formed and trade became highly organized. Whatever the origin of the word "check," which has been associated by some scholars with the Chinese who brought them to the Near East as paper money in the Mongol period, an institution similar to letters of credit and notes existed in the tenth century. It was not safe to carry large sums of money on one's person, hence to transfer funds from one city to another, one had recourse to a banker *(sarraf)* in one city who issued a check on his colleague in the other city. Some sources tell how such "checks" written in the western part of the Islamic world

were honored in the eastern part. The same procedure continued in use to the present, as experienced by the author
in traveling from Herat to Mashhad in 1943.

We have mentioned the armed peasants, who were especially prominent in mountainous areas of Central Asia. This
was less true in the more organized oasis of Bukhara, which
was protected by the well-trained professional army of the
Samanid *amir*. As the power and importance of the soldiers
grew, so did the independence and influence of the peasantry,
however little, decline. The *dihqans* too changed, in that
they became more involved in trade and crafts as well as
land, and they gradually moved to the cities. In the oasis
of Bukhara, the *dihqans* more and more came to the capital
and lived near the court as absentee landlords.

One study which has not been made, but would be of
interest, is to determine how much of the *dihqan* class was
pre-Islamic in origin, how much was Arab in origin, and
how many were *nouveaux riches*. In one city of Khurasan
in Seljük times, over half of the forty odd important land-
owning families were Arab in origin, three traced their
descent to Sasanian families, and the rest were high officials
in the bureaucracy, with an odd merchant. Perhaps among
the leading families in Bukhara the merchants and bureaucrats were proportionally more numerous, but the proportion
of the Arab to Iranian element must have been similar to
that in the town of Baihaq.

The bureaucracy has been mentioned several times, and,
of course, the government officials for the most part lived
in the cities. One may divide them into two principal classes,
the secular clerks or scribes *(dabir)* and the religious officials

(faqih). Although there was a semblance of continuity in the
scribal class, there was nothing like a civil service, and
many officials lost their positions when a *vezir* was dis-
graced and a new one appointed. Patronage was rampant,
and a new *vezir* usually had a complete apparatus of functionaries who moved in and took over the jobs of the out-
going administration. The unemployed scribes were a problem: they intrigued to regain their positions or sought the
patronage of some powerful governor or minister of state.
The offices were usually passed on from father to son in
apprentice fashion and, of course, tricks of the trade were
well guarded secrets. It seems that the later guilds were not
yet important.

The religious bureaucracy was parallel to the civil organization, and it would seem much more stable. Since all legal
problems were decided by religious judges *(qadis)*, the
number and influence of the religious officials was very
great. The *qadi* handled cases of litigation, criminal acts,
except certain political offenses, and all problems of personal law. The mosque was usually the site for the passing
of judgments, although we hear of judgment being passed
in homes of the *qadis*. Unfortunately details about the pro-
cedures are lacking. The Sunni clergy in Bukhara was especially influential, for it was their leaders who first invited
Isma'il into Bukhara, and later, sometime after the fall of
the Samanids, they assumed the political as well as the social
leadership of the city.

There were many famous *faqihs,* or men learned in Islamic
religious law, and each prominent leader had followers and
students. Public opinion played a great role in legal decisions,

undoubtedly many times unjustly, but the thinking of the *'ulama,* or learned savants of Islamic jurisprudence, was being organized into an institution which paralleled the civil government. Under the Samanids, the organs of the state and the *'ulama* usually co-operated closely, although the people came to regard the religious leaders as protectors against the tyranny of the state. In cases of public unrest or demonstrations, the clergy could not be counted as sure supporters of the government. The wide jurisdiction of the religious institution insured a check on many activities of the state in its various domains.

It should be noted that many Muslim savants regarded the office of judge with great distaste, even excusing themselves from appointments to such offices, which were made by the civil authorities. The Samanid period, however, is one of transition, for the judges, although paid by the state, came into higher repute. Much could be written about the development of jurisprudence and its relation to theology, but this is not the place for such discussion.

It would be wrong to assume that Bukhara was free from theological disputes, the most important of which was engendered by the Mu'tazilite "free thinkers" of early tenth-century Baghdad. The Sufis, or mystics, so prominent in later Iran, were beginning to organize themselves in the tenth century, and again Bukhara was an important center for them. These theologians, if one may use the word in a very general sense, were far apart from the students of jurisprudence who had come to dominate Islamic philosophy and theology by the tenth century. The great collections of traditions of the Prophet, on which Islamic jurisprudence and

76

theology were based, had been finished before the tenth century. So it was not unexpected that other areas of religious thought would more and more occupy men's minds in the time under consideration and later.

It is, of course, impossible to go into any detail about the great developments in the religion of Islam in the tenth century, but it was a time of change. For example, higher criticism of readings of the Quran and methods of testing the reliability of traditions were elaborated by savants in this century. Every province had its school of Quran readers, and every word and accent of the text was taken very seriously, even to the point of violent and sanguinary disputes. In Bukhara, the Hanafite school of jurisprudence prevailed, although another school, the Shafi'ites, existed elsewhere in Transoxiana.

All of the above is only briefly mentioned to indicate the richness of thought and intellectual activity in the tenth century Islamic world. Bukhara, as the Samanid capital, fully participated in the variegated activities of the Muslim savants and bureaucrats. A caveat remains, however, in that the sources tell about conditions in Baghdad much more fully than elsewhere, and one cannot be sure that a parallel in Bukhara is always valid. Furthermore, notices about certain affairs in Nishapur or Samarqand, important cities of the Samanid domain, may not equally apply to the capital Bukhara. We have only scattered notices about life in the various cities of eastern Iran, and since our focus is Bukhara we must be careful of imputing a situation found in a provincial city by analogy to the capital. For example, both Shi'ite sectarians and the Karamiyya, a sect founded by a certain Ibn

Karram in the time of the Tahirids, remained strong in Nishapur throughout the Samanid period but not, it would seem, in Bukhara.

To turn to another area, the arts under the Samanids, we also find a flourishing of previous traditions combined with a new Islamic taste to form an Iranian-Islamic art of high quality and sophistication. From the available evidence, it would seem that ancient motifs in the arts persisted generally longer in eastern Iran than in the west. It is very difficult to differentiate Central Asian features in the art forms of Iran in Islamic times, primarily because of the paucity of art objects, and, of course, the inability to assign certain objects to a definite place of origin. We may assume that the artistic heritage of the Kushans in eastern Iran continued into Islamic times, and the conquering Arabs were correct in their designation of Transoxiana, "the land beyond the river," as a cultural and political area distinct from Sasanian Iran. The increasing number of excavations and finds of Islamic art objects in Soviet Central Asia are confirming the picture derived from written sources, that the arts of the Samanid period represented an amalgam of indigenous traditions, Sasanian Iranian influences, mainly from the early Islamic period, and a new Islamic art which developed under the 'Abbasids. The last is best represented by the finds made in the temporary 'Abbasid capital of Samarra, after which it is generally called the Samarra style.

To begin with the Samarra style, in decoration it is characterized by curved surfaces in planes of high and low relief, perfect for the media of plaster and stucco. The so-called tomb of *amir* Isma'il, but better called the mausoleum of the

Samanids, in Bukhara shows affinities with Samarra, but it also suggests a wood original in that the decoration or design is accentuated by multiple, angular planes of high and low relief rather than curved surfaces. In its architecture, the structure shows affinities to the fire temple of the variety known in Iran as *chahar taq,* or four arches covered with a low dome. The most prominent antecedents, however, are the Central Asian, pre-Islamic palaces and villas excavated in Varakhsha and several sites in ancient Khwarazm, modern Khiva. Indeed, the mausoleum of the Samanids in Bukhara is a fine example of the mingling of three influences. As such it may be called distinctively Samanid or Bukharan.

Because of climatic conditions, the usual form of construction in Central Asia was stamped mud, or adobe, in the houses. Both sun- and kiln-dried bricks were employed on larger, public buildings, and plaster usually covered them on the inside. Varied and more sophisticated solutions for putting a circular dome on a square building had replaced the old pre-Islamic stepped vaults on the corners. The architecture of the Samanids, it would appear, was well developed and a forerunner of the elaborate structures in Bukhara and Samarqand of the Timurid period in the fifteenth century.

Woodwork seems to have been an art which was also distinctively Central Asian or even Samanid. In any event, it flourished primarily in the mountain areas of Central Asia and present-day Afghanistan down to recent times. The intricate carving of floral designs on wood was copied later in stone, and we have several superb examples of tombstones from a later period obviously based on wooden originals. Some beautiful carved wooden doors from the Samanid period have survived and are in museums in the former U.S.S.R. It is probable that purely Islamic structures, such as mosques and minarets, had profuse decorations, although none of the structures from the Samanid period mentioned in literary sources have survived.

Although Islam frowned upon representations of animals or humans, such representations did not cease in Iran, any more than did the drinking of wine. Nonetheless, abstract, geometric patterns and floral designs received a new impetus and great expansion under Islam. The Sunni religious leaders of the Hanafite school of law, whose role has been noted, strongly encouraged the use of decoration and patterns rather than forms of living creatures. The progressive geometricization of art, if one may so designate it, was especially evident in the decoration of buildings and on pottery.

The pottery of Samanid times is known chiefly from excavations in Samarqand and Nishapur. Usually a bold or striking decoration painted in a colored slip under a transparent lead glaze characterizes the pottery of this period. The use of decorative Kufic Arabic inscriptions, or designs resembling writing, are most typical of this ware, although floral patterns and even stylized birds and animals are to be found. This ware is found in museums under the rubric of Afrasiab ware, so-named after the local designation of the old city of Samarqand where such pottery was first found. The Samanid ceramics were varied in design and manifold in techniques, and it is impossible here to discuss the many interesting details about them.

Central Asian ceramic ware has been found in various sites in the Near East, evidence of the popularity of Samanid pottery. The forms of pottery were also by no means uniform; pitchers, flat plates, bowls, animal or even human figures used as pitchers, a man on horseback, and others, indicate their interesting variety. Perhaps a certain puritan opposition to the use of gold and silver for household implements or tools spurred the artists in their embellishment of clay and bronze vessels. Whether this was the prime cause of the extraordinary development of pottery techniques such as enamel, lustre ware, gold leaf, and of elaborate designs, we do not know. But medieval Islamic pottery achieved very high standards of technical as well as artistic excellence. Chinese influences, of great importance later, can be detected also in the copying of porcelain by Samanid artists. Here, as in all the arts, one must distinguish between luxury products and everyday kitchen ware, just as court poetry must be distinguished from popular poetry. Bronze followed the traditions of pottery, although the persistence of Sasanian motifs was perhaps stronger in this medium than in others.

Several elaborately decorated bronze kettles and ewers from Central Asia from the post-Samanid period have survived, but they give evidence of highly developed techniques already in the earlier period. In metal work in general, such as armor and weapons, Samarqand was a noted center. In other minor arts, such as weaving and textiles, the Samanid domains were pre-eminent in the Islamic world. It is of interest that the earliest dated piece of silk weaving from Islamic Iran, from the church of St. Josse, Pas-de-Calais but now in the Louvre, was made for the governor of Khurasan under the successor of the *amir* Nuh b. Nasr about 958.

Music developed much as did the other arts; under Islam

a mixture of Arab and Iranian elements took place. The pre-Islamic Persians were noted for their achievements and skill in music, and many instruments used in the Islamic world were Sasanian or even earlier Iranian in origin. The Tahirids were known as patrons of music, and several descendants of the Tahirids, probably at the court in Bukhara, wrote tracts on music. Indeed, some of the greatest intellects of the age, such as al-Farabi and al-Razi (Rhazes) studied and wrote about music, while Rudaki already has been mentioned. From the various writings we learn that in Samanid times some of the melodies or modes of music current in the Sasanid empire were still popular many centuries later. In the Samanid period, a new instrument, the *shahrud,* perhaps a kind of harp, was said to have been invented in Samarqand in 912, adding to the already numerous company of instruments such as the lute, pandore, viol, etc. From the writings of Ibn Sina, we learn of differences between Iranian and Arab music, the former being richer. Arab music was appreciated and copied in the world of Iran as well as the native music, whereas the reverse was less true in the Arabic speaking parts of the caliphate. Just as with wine and painting, music was also defended by the Iranians against more puritanical Arab tendencies.

The queen of the arts, painting, presents difficulties again because of general disapproving Islamic sentiments. We must look to wall paintings or to book illustrations for our conception of Samanid painting. Three human figures of the Samanid period, discovered on wall paintings in Afrasiab in 1913, unfortunately were lost through disintegration before being copied. Wall paintings from Lashgari Bazar in southern Afghanistan, from the later Ghaznavid period, reveal that paintings of human forms in life size did not offend the reputedly fanatic Muslim Ghaznavid rulers. Since pre-Islamic wall paintings have been found in Varakhsha, Panjikant and elsewhere in Transoxiana, the continuance of the tradition in Islamic times is not surprising. The techniques are similar and the subjects, hunting scenes and banquet scenes, also attest to the continuity from pre-Islamic times. Even in articles of dress, such as elaborate, decorated silk jackets and coats, boots, and pointed hats characteristic of the Sogdians, there is a continuity. The last was mentioned by the Turkish nomad rulers of the seventh century in their runic inscriptions in Mongolia, and may have influenced the tall, pointed cap of Muslim savants called the *qalansua,* first attested in eastern Iran.

Calligraphy was highly developed in the Iranian part of the Islamic world, and the various kinds of decorated Kufic Arabic script again attest to the high quality of artists in the east. It seems that miniatures and illumination in books were special features of pre-Islamic Manichaean books, although some ancient Zoroastrian books are also said to have been decorated. There is a story that when a Chinese princess came to Bukhara in the time of Nasr as a bride for his son Nuh, she brought with her an artist who made the illustrations of Rudaki's translation of Kalila and Dimna. Whether this story is true or not, it serves to illustrate the wide flung connections of the Samanids in the art fields as well as others. Certainly Chinese influences on later Persian miniature painting are obvious, but one need not assume that they began only with the Mongol invasions of the late twelfth century. Indeed the fame of Iran as a center of art has persisted down the ages, and Bukhara was part of the world of Iran.

So Bukhara under Nasr b. Ahmad played a leading role in the process of creating an ecumenical Islamic culture in all domains from religion and law to music and pottery. But in making of Islam a world religion and civilization the door was opened to variety and to new fields of endeavor, which by some students have been described as the instruments of the decline of Islam. Some scholars extol the golden age of the 'Abbasids in the ninth century, when the Arabic language reigned supreme and Arab mores theoretically still influenced society. But they forget that even then, the inevitable forces of change were at work. Arab scholars frequently blame the Iranians for "disrupting" Islam by seeking to use Persian in place of Arabic and by promoting old Iranian practices and traditions in the Islamic world. The *Shu'ubiyya* certainly existed, for chauvinists are to be found in every time and clime, but to condemn all Iranians as anti-Arab, hence *ipso facto* anti-Islamic, is not only absurd but unjust to those persons at the court of the Samanids who sought to enrich Islam and make it really a multi-national, multi-linguistic, and variegated cultural entity, not bound to exalted bedouin mores or imagined legitimate Islamic practices derived from Arab customs. In this great endeavor those subjects of the Samanids proved to be realistic, and they pointed the way to the future.

· 5 ·

The Silver Age

The most noble horse on coming to
Bukhara becomes like an ass.
ABU MANSUR AL-'ABDUNI

IF WE FOLLOW certain conventions of history, we may use
the term "silver age" to describe the last decades of Samanid
rule. Not that any such designation satisfies the investigator
in all respects, nor even that the divisions in time are little
more than arbitrary; but one must erect a framework of
perspective on the past, and one can detect seeds of decline
in the reigns of Nuh b. Nasr and his successor. The artistic,
scientific, and cultural life of Bukhara continued to flourish
and even in some respects shone brighter than previously,
but the high point of the city of Bukhara had passed. With
the Ghaznavids and then the Seljüks, the center of power and
influence was no longer in Transoxiana but in the west and
south.

The new king Nuh b. Nasr (943–954) had to face financial difficulties shortly after his accession, some of them
engendered by the generosity of the former ruler as well
as the plundering of the treasury in 942 to pacify the rebels
against the *amir* Nasr. There is information that in his first
year taxes were levied twice in order to obtain necessary
funds for the bureaucracy. The royal guards and some of the
regular army did not receive their pay for a long period, and

85

this contributed greatly to unrest. Unfortunately, the new prime minister, Muhammad al-Sulami, was a *faqih* who was a conservative, even fanatically religious man, tending to pay more attention to his personal devotions than to the affairs of state. He had been appointed to placate those who deplored the "heretical" views of the *amir* Nasr.

A new problem for the Samanids was the rise of a strong Shi'ite dynasty in western Iran called the Boyids, who vied with the Samanids for the control of Rayy and central Iran. Previously the Samanid armies had been able to maintain at least the nominal authority of their princes in the Caspian provinces and in central Iran (Hamadan–Rayy–Damghan). In 944 the governor of Khurasan, Abu 'Ali Chaghani, a scion of an ancient feudal family from the mountainous area of present day Tajikistan, revolted against Nuh when the latter sought to replace him with Ibrahim b. Simjur, who was a favorite of the Turkish guards. Abu 'Ali was an influential person who would not accept his removal and revolted. He sought the help of Nuh's uncle Ibrahim b. Ahmad, and the two prepared to carry the flag of rebellion to the gates of Bukhara.

Meanwhile affairs of state had deteriorated in Bukhara under the indifferent *vezir*. The end result of various intrigues and opposition to the *vezir* was a rising of the military leaders who seized al-Sulami and put him to death. The army then refused to fight against Abu 'Ali. When the latter approached Bukhara, *amir* Nuh fled to Samarqand. The rebels entered the capital and Ibrahim b. Ahmad was proclaimed the new *amir*. The rule of Abu 'Ali and Ibrahim was not popular, however, and after two months Abu 'Ali left to return to his homeland in Chaghaniyan. Ibrahim became reconciled with Nuh and agreed to the latter's reinstatement as *amir*. Nuh returned to Bukhara where he shortly broke his promise by seizing and blinding his uncle, together with some of his followers. The troubles in Khurasan, however, were far from ended and Samanid rule there was never the same until the end of the dynasty.

The historical sources dwell in some detail on the military events in Khurasan and on the changing fortunes of the Samanids and the Boyids. More important than the latter for the government in Bukhara, however, were internal revolts. The last fifty years of Samanid rule saw all of the provinces south of the Oxus draw away from allegiance to Bukhara. Symptomatic of the growing internal weakness of the state was the rapid change in *vezirs*. From 954–59, there were four prime ministers in succession. Power actually had passed from the civil administration to the military, and one of the Turkish generals, Alptigin, held the greatest influence in Bukhara in Nuh's reign. The rise of the Turks, however, is part of a historical process which changed the face of the countryside, and discussion of this is reserved for the next chapter.

Outside of the capital, the figure of Abu 'Ali Chaghani dominates the reign of Nuh, for in 952 he was reappointed governor of Khurasan and waged war against the Boyids. Over a year later he made peace with them, but Nuh disapproved and removed him from his office. The *amir* died shortly afterwards, in the late summer of 954, and was succeeded by his son 'Abd al-Malik, who continued in the footsteps of his father, even more dominated by the military

87

party. 'Abd al-Malik did make one rather feeble attempt to rid himself of military control but failed. After several changes in prime ministers, the candidate of the military party, Abu 'Ali b. Muhammad al-Bal'ami, son of the earlier *vezir,* was appointed to the same post. Unfortunately the son did not have the qualities of his father and was a puppet of the generals and especially of Alptigin, who continued as the power behind the throne. Intrigues, bribery, and sheer force more and more prevailed among the highest officials of the state. Gardizi, a later historian, says that 'Abd al-Malik frequently played polo, but one day he had drunk too much wine and was unable to control his horse, which threw him and broke his neck. This was in the autumn of 961.

The immediate consequence of the sudden death of the *amir* was disorder among the populace. A new palace in Bukhara built by 'Abd al-Malik was sacked and burned by a mob. After some uncertainty, Abu Salih Mansur b. Nuh, brother of 'Abd al-Malik, was named ruler by the acclamation of the royal guard. Everyone rallied to him save Alptigin, who previously had been appointed governor of Khurasan. Seeing himself isolated, Alptigin left Nishapur, the provincial capital, and made his way to Ghazna, where he took over rule from a native dynast and thus laid the foundations for the later Ghaznavid Empire.

It is appropriate here to clarify briefly the titles *sipahsalar,* "commander of the army," and *amir* of Khurasan which appear in the sources. The Samanids themselves after Isma'il, as successors of the Tahirids, were originally *amirs* of Khurasan, but since they resided in Transoxiana or *ma wara'l-nahr,* "above the river," instead of in Nishapur, *ma duna'l-nahr,*

88

"below the river," they appointed the commander of the Samanid army to govern the land "below the river." So in Alptigin's time, he was the commander of the army, which meant he also governed the land "below the river" from Nishapur, the provincial capital of Khurasan. The sources unfortunately sometimes are confusing in their designation of the *amir* of Khurasan, since on the one hand it could mean the Samanid ruler in Bukhara, or his army commander, governor of the land "below the river."

It appears that the contemporary, as well as later, historians discerned what we see from a distance, that the center of gravity and power had left Transoxiana to move westward to Nishapur, Rayy, and Isfahan. For Bukhara was no longer important as the Samanid capital; more was decided in Nishapur, center of the province of Khurasan, and the chronicles tell of events there, and even in Seistan, more than in Bukhara. The star of the Boyids was rising fast and they too became known for patronage of scholarship and the arts. Still, the fame of "the kings of the east," as they are called in contemporary sources, remained high among the writers. The geographer al-Maqdisi, who flourished in the second half of the tenth century, wrote that "they are the best of kings in character, appearance, and respect for science and men of science . . . . Among their usages, they do not require men of learning to fall on the ground before them, and they hold assemblies in the evenings during the month of Ramadan for discussions in the presence of the ruler."

Mansur b. Nuh continued in the happy tradition of his predecessors as a patron of the arts and learning. His *vezirs,* Abu Ja'far 'Utbi and Bal'ami tried to recreate the age of

Nasr, but it was much more difficult. In the last year of
Mansur's reign, Abu 'Abdallah Ahmad b. Muhammad Jaihani, grandson of the famous Jaihani, became *vezir*. So the
descendants of the famous early Samanid *vezirs* took up the
reins of state, but unfortunately none were the men their
forefathers were.

Mansur reigned fifteen years and died in the summer of
976, leaving the throne to his son Nuh II, who was only
thirteen years old. Real power was assumed by a capable new
prime minister Abu'l-Husain 'Utbi, who sought to restore
the influence of the bureaucracy against the military leaders.
For a short time he seemed to be successful, since he was
able to place his friends in high military offices. But a dis-
astrous campaign against the Boyids in 982 forced the ener-
getic *vezir* to take military affairs into his own hands, and
the resulting opposition brought about his murder in Merv
shortly afterwards. With his death the last influential and
effective prime minister passed from the Samanid scene.
Succeeding *vezirs* no longer had the authority to keep order
in the Samanid domains, which in effect were limited to
Transoxiana, since the provinces south of the Oxus River
were in the hands of practically independent governors.
The financial affairs of the kingdom were also in disorder.
The entry of a Turkish army from the east into Bukhara
in 992 really marked the end of the dynasty, although the
Samanids managed to regain the capital and maintain a
precarious rule until the end of the century.

The second half of the tenth century saw the decline of
the *dihqan* class, the backbone of Bukharan society. Al-

though the process of deterioration lasted more than half a century and had manifold causes, one of the prime reasons for the change was the rise of the cities and the flowering of city life. We have already mentioned the migration of the *dihqans* to the cities, a process confirmed by archaeology. The number of villas or castles in various parts of the oasis of Bukhara, so great in pre-Samanid times, became negligible by the end of Samanid rule. The centralization of authority in the Samanid bureaucracy, of course, contributed to the weakening of power in the *dihqan* class. The consequences of its loss of influence and power were far-reaching, not the least of which was its role in the prelude to the Turkification of Transoxiana.

The economic problems of the state were matched by an economic crisis among the people. From Narshakhi and other authors it would appear that land values in the oasis declined throughout the Samanid period. There are some indications that the desert encroached on the western area of the oasis, perhaps in part the result of the abandonment of the great walls, which were not repaired or in any way maintained. Since the land holdings of the Samanid family steadily increased, which in effect meant that state lands increased, the financial troubles of the state were reflected on the land, which was not maintained as it should have been. Another category of land holdings which increased in extent were the *waqf* lands or religious endowments, attached to a mausoleum, a mosque, a dervish center, or the like. In comparison, the third large category of land holdings, of the *dihqans,* decreased. New landowners included merchants, religious leaders, and military officers; and it was only natural that the traditional, lineage-conscious, old aristocracy should give way before new owners.

The tax problems of earlier times, between Muslims and non-Muslims, had been settled, but during the Samanid period the practice of granting tax-free lands or freedom from paying taxes, to *sayyids,* descendants of the prophet, favorites of the ruler, and officers of the guard, did not help the coffers of the state.

Naturally the peasantry bore the increased weight of the government's need for larger taxes. To escape such burdens, when they could, sons of peasants found their way to the cities, just as did the *dihqans.* Although Muslims were not supposed to own other Muslims as slaves, household slaves did exist, mainly recruited from pagan Turks or inhabitants of the mountains east of the Zarafshan River. Women took up many of the burdens of slaves, for they worked in weaving and spinning establishments and elsewhere in the bazaars. The peasants were very little different from the serfs of Medieval Europe.

The striking feature of later Samanid rule was the development of the city into that structure which it was to maintain down to the twentieth century. Bukhara, as the capital, led the way, but other cities were similar in their growth. The large square to the west of the citadel of Bukhara, called the Rigistan, became the administrative center of the city and state, with the buildings of the various *divans,* palaces of the *amirs,* and other structures built around it. To the northwest of the Rigistan was the quarter of the residences of the aristocracy, where, according to Narshakhi, land was very expensive. The central part of Bukhara was occupied by the bazaars, divided into various quarters of specialties, coppersmiths, rug makers, shoe makers, etc. The bazaars were self-contained in that raw materials were brought into them, and artisans, who mostly lived behind their shops, made articles which were sold by merchants. The bazaars in the various cities were quite similar and linked together by merchants who maintained establishments in several centers.

Poets and other writers complained about the dirt, stench, and crowded conditions in the city of Bukhara under the later Samanids. The growth in population had not been matched either by expansion of public responsibility or by government regulations, and hygienic conditions in the crowded, squalid living quarters were bad enough to rouse protests. Garbage was thrown into the narrow streets outside of high mud walls, and lanes and streets were sometimes almost impassable. The maze of dank, dark alleys reflected the concern of the citizen of Bukhara to retreat into his private dwelling, leaving the world outside to take care of itself. Just as in the growth of cities in western Europe in the later Middle Ages, so in the domains of the Samanids, cities such as Bukhara, Samarqand, and Nishapur became centers of disease and pestilence. The aristocracy was able to escape the city and go to summer houses in gardens near Bukhara, but the masses were caught in their small rooms on narrow streets. Poems have been preserved which describe Bukhara in this period as a sewer, unfit for human life.

When economic conditions were bad, unemployment rose and city mobs were ever ready to revolt. We find echoes of such unrest in brief notices about the cities of the Samanid kingdom, but the writers of histories, it must be remembered, were usually members of the upper classes or writing for patrons among the aristocracy or for rulers, so popular movements are not well described. Another class of people who must have been a source of unrest and trouble were the *ghazis,* or warriors of the faith, who came from all over the Islamic world to wage holy war against the infidel Turks of Central Asia. With the conversion of many Turkish tribes, in the tenth century, however, the reason for such *ghazis* to exist vanished. Many turned to banditry or swelled the unruly city mobs.

One of the great scourges of cities in Medieval Europe, fire, was also frequently present in Samanid Bukhara. Several sources tell of the frequency of conflagrations in the city which had much wood construction. Narshakhi tells how the residence of the *amir* Mansur b. Nuh in Bukhara at the Rigistan caught fire by accident when the people started a bonfire according to an ancient custom. Sparks fell on the roof and the palace was completely destroyed. Some buildings were several stories high, veritable fire traps in case of a serious fire.

The population of Bukhara in this period is quite unknown, and any estimates, by contemporary sources or modern scholars, are pure guesswork. From archaeological investigations plus comparisons with other cities, one might hazard a guess that the population was over one hundred thousand, but estimates reaching from one half to one million are surely exaggerated.

The literate, or rather more accurately the literary, class

94

was small, even though it made a great impression in history, if not so much in the contemporary world of the tenth century. Life was too hard for the vast majority to be able to indulge in the higher pursuits of leisure. As we have noted, most literature was produced for the court, but the second half of the tenth century saw some significant productions, especially the Iranian epic.

Abu Mansur Muhammad b. Ahmad Daqiqi was the principal poet who appeared on the scene about a decade after Rudaki and flourished under Mansur b. Nuh. His birthplace is unknown but he first composed poetry in the provincial court of Chaghaniyan. Then, like Rudaki, he was invited to Bukhara, where he was later commissioned by the new *amir* Nuh b. Mansur to write the epic story of pre-Islamic Iran in verse. He composed about a thousand verses, but about 977 he was murdered, according to some sources, by his own slave. Firdosi later incorporated the verses of Daqiqi, mostly dealing with the life and times of the prophet Zoroaster, into his version of the *Shah Name* or "Book of Kings." Daqiqi is said to have been a Zoroastrian himself, but this is unlikely in spite of his praise of the ancient faith and of wine. Perhaps Daqiqi was a partisan of the *Shu'ubiyya* or an ardent Iranophile, but there is no good evidence that he was a Zoroastrian. Furthermore, some lyrics attributed to him were written under the prevailing strong Arabic influence, both in style and vocabulary, quite distinct from the archaic style of the epic.

The successor of Daqiqi was Abu'l-Qasim Firdosi who brought the epic to completion. Firdosi was born in or near the city of Tus in Khurasan, not far from modern Mashhad.

The date of his birth is uncertain but probably it was between 932 and 936, when the Samanids were at the height of their power. He came from a *dihqan* family and was raised in the traditions of this class. We are not concerned here about the life of Firdosi or his relations with Mahmud of Ghazna, son of Sebüktigin of the Ghaznavid dynasty, but rather we should examine his great epic in the framework of the society and beliefs of the time. A "Book of Kings," or *Khwatai Name,* had existed in Pahlavi from Sasanian times, apparently a history of Iran from the legendary, heroic pre-Sasanian period down almost to the end of the Sasanian dynasty. Several translations of this work were made into Arabic, but only excerpts of the various Arabic versions are found in general world histories in Arabic. Incomplete versions in prose and verse apparently also existed in New Persian before the time of Firdosi, but his main source seems to have been a "book of kings" in prose compiled by several persons requested by the feudal lord of Tus, Abu Mansur Muhammad b. 'Abd al-Razzaq, which was completed in 957. It was the genius of Firdosi which brought together the verses of Daqiqi, folk traditions and songs, and information from prose sources, into a unified poetic book which became the national epic of Iran. It alone became the national epic because the city civilization required a written, fixed, and one might say, a sophisticated, polished poem rather than the varied compositions of bards or minstrels reciting the lays of the heroes of ancient Iran to the knights or *dihqans* in their nocturnal gatherings. I believe that Firdosi, although reflecting the literary taste and interest of the *dihqan* class, composed his poem for the court, the city folk, and for other poets who would criticize his skill, and thus did what the other Persian poets had done or were doing. Firdosi brought the epic into the Islamic Iranian society of his time with the literary canons and the interests of his contemporaries in mind. So his *Shah Name* has survived, in the opinion of many, as the greatest literary production of the New Persian language or of Islamic Iran.

The sources of Firdosi were many and varied and it is not easy to distinguish them in his *Shah Name*. It has been proposed that Firdosi knew Pahlavi and mainly drew upon this knowledge for his writing, but it is most unlikely that he was so equipped. Narshakhi and others told of popular songs or dirges on the death of Siyavush, an ancient hero, perhaps mythical, who according to legend lived in Bukhara. We may assume that such pieces were incorporated into the *Shah Name,* but the question arises whether the style and the verse metre of the *Shah Name* were created by Daqiqi or some other poet of the Samanid period. One may suggest that, regardless whether the metre of the *Shah Name,* called *Mutaqarib,* was derived from an Arabic or a Middle Persian prototype, it was not a folk form but a literary creation. The *Shah Name* was not written as a folk epic, taken verbatim from the mouths of minstrels; it is rather a polished literary poem. What may we say of the contents of the Iranian national epic?

Many books have been written about Firdosi's *Shah Name,* and it is idle here to discuss the work in any detail. I believe it is important to emphasize the unity which Firdosi brought to disparate elements of the heroic past of the Iranian peoples. For only in the time of the Samanids could a unified epic arise in the new consciousness of the unity of Iran and its history. Under the Sasanians, Bukhara and Trans-oxiana were not part of Iran, even though the mystique of an Iranian *ecumene* must have survived the world empire of the Achaemenids. The dream or fiction of a unified empire of Iran from the beginning of history down to the Arab conquests is the central thread of the *Shah Name*. But how conscious was the feeling of unity of all Iranians before the time of the Samanids? In pre-Islamic times, did Manichaean Sogdians consider themselves blood brothers of Zoroastrians from Fars province, politically separated but hopefully someday to be united under one king of kings of all Iran? One suspects that such beliefs were mainly found in Sasanian royal or aristocratic circles, and that the real spread of such sentiments came primarily in Islamic times with the expansion of New Persian as the *lingua franca* of all Iranians, and the fusing of Persian, Sogdian, Khwarazmian, and other local traditions into a general, synthetic all-Iranian, but Islamic, tradition. By this I do not mean to deny the reality of a continuing memory of an ancient political and religious (Zoroastrian) unity of all Iranians, but it seems to have blossomed with new force and spread especially in the tenth century A.D. among the Iranian peoples everywhere.

Firdosi then reflected beautifully the beliefs and sentiments of his own age. In a general but descriptive sense he provided a psychiatric treatment for the problems of his contemporaries who had to deal with a conflict of Islam and Iran. He resurrected the memory of a heroic past and gave a unified personality to the Iranian, who found that he could reconcile Zoroaster and Muhammad and be richer for having both. Firdosi in his epic gave a unity to the disparate lineage of the Iranian, and thus matched the Arab with his oneness of purpose derived from the prophet Muhammad. One might compare the Muslim Iranian with the Japanese who followed both Buddhism and Shinto, reconciling any conflicts; but such parallels may be misleading. The importance of Firdosi as the forger of a document of Iranian unity and nationalism cannot be minimized, and his work is fascinating because of this, as well as its literary interest.

The *Shah Name* has been characterized as a chain of chronologically arranged episodes in the lives of various Iranian heroes. One of the motifs expressed in various parts of the work is the conflict of good and evil with the final victory of good, and as part of this struggle the opposition of Iran and Turan. In Firdosi's time this meant the conflict between Iranians and Turks, although it was probably originally a struggle between the sown and the steppe. Loyalty of a man to his family or relatives, or a vassal to his lord or king, is another motif of the epic. Revenge, the need for a king to be righteous above all else, and the charisma of kingly glory, or *farr,* are all elements in the various episodes of the book. An analysis of such scenes as the mortal conflict of father and son would require much study, and the *Shah Name* is filled with the stuff of which sagas and epics are made.

It has been recognized that most of the mythical pre-Sasanian part of the *Shah Name* is east Iranian in origin, and we have mentioned Siyavush and his connection with Bukhara. Perhaps the real hero of the work is Rustam, who is supposed to have come from Seistan. He was quite possibly a Saka hero, and the fact that many of the parallel epic books in New Persian, such as the *Garshasp Name* and the *Barzu Name,* are concerned with what might be called the Seistan epic cycle, or the family of Rustam, shows the importance of that province in the whole Iranian epic tradition. Some scholars have postulated a Khwarazmian cycle of tales, a Sogdian, and others which together with the Seistan cycle were combined to form the *Shah Name,* but evidence for this is lacking, although it may be partially true.

It has been pointed out also many times that the *Shah Name* was really written for the Samanids, but their rule ended before Firdosi finished his work, and he turned then to Mahmud of Ghazna for patronage. The pretensions of the Samanids to lineage from the ancient kings of Iran, their struggle with the Turkish nomads, and their support of the *dihqans,* all point to the thesis that the Samanids were the legitimate heirs of the Sasanians in Firdosi's time. Firdosi, who probably died in 1020 (or 1025), saw the victory of the Turks, but he might have foreseen that they would be conquered by Iranian culture. And so Firdosi's work has remained to the present as the symbol of Iranian nationalism, shared by present day Persians, Afghans and Tajiks, as well as by other smaller Iranian groups.

It is interesting and significant to note that the cultural reconciliation of Islam and Iran was achieved in eastern Iran and Transoxiana before it was in western Iran. In the realm of the Boyids there was also what has been called by some savants an "Iranian renaissance," but it took a somewhat different path than in the east. In western Iran, the old heart of the Sasanian Empire, the Pahlavi language, Zoroastrian religion, and Sasanian traditions were all stronger than in the east. Pahlavi continued to be used in the eleventh century, as attested by inscriptions on buildings, in the Caspian provinces, together with Arabic. Furthermore, in the ninth and early tenth centuries there was a revival of literary activity among the Zoroastrian priests, especially under several tolerant and intellectually curious caliphs in Baghdad. Iranian aspirations and traditions were too closely bound up with the past in western Iran, and Zoroastrianism was still alive if hardly flourishing. The climate for a "renaissance" was much better in the east.

The spirit of the Samanid achievement did, however, spread to the west, but it is of interest that the west Iranian versions of the epic, which were in prose, were based primarily on Pahlavi sources, whereas Firdosi's work was not. One of the west Iranian versions was called the *Gird Name* by a certain Rustam Larijani, who was a contemporary of Firdosi at the court of the Boyid ruler of Hamadan. Another version was written by Firuzan, a royal tutor at the court of a ruler of Isfahan called Shams al-Mulk Faramurz (1041–51). So Iranian nationalism was in the air all over the Iranian world, but only in the Samanid domains did the "winning combination" come into existence with Firdosi and survive as the "canonical version" of the national epic.

If we examine the sources regarding the centers of translation from Pahlavi into Arabic in the eighth and ninth centuries, other than the capital of the caliphate Baghdad, we find a seeming correspondence with centers of New Persian literary activity. The centers were Isfahan, Istakhr–Shiraz, and in the east, to a much lesser degree, Merv. Although we

have insufficient information, one might conjecture that these
cities were centers of translators, who in an earlier epoch
translated from Pahlavi to Arabic to suit the demands of
the age, whereas in a later period other translators turned
Arabic into New Persian according to the wishes of the rulers
and aristocracy of that time. Merv was important in the east
since it was the capital of the Arab garrisons in Khurasan,
as it had been the military center of the Sasanian frontier in
the east. Under the Samanids, Merv remained important,
although Bukhara and Nishapur surpassed her.

Just as we concentrated on poetry when speaking of the
early Samanids, so under the later Samanids poetry, and
especially the epic, usurped the stage. But in the later period
Persian prose comes into prominence and New Persian be-
gins to develop from a language "fit only for tales of Chosroes
and bed-time stories," according to al-Biruni, into a manifold instrument of scientific and philosophical literature as
well. We have already mentioned the obvious need of writing missionary tracts in the Persian language understood by
most people in Iran and Transoxiana, when speaking of the
Isma'ili missions. To combat heresy a Sunni religious leader,
Abu'l-Qasim Samarqandi (died 954) wrote a religious work
on orthodox Islam in Arabic, and at the request of the Samanid *amir* (probably Nuh b. Nasr), translated it into Persian.
The earliest New Persian prose works were translated from
Arabic originals and only later did independent compositions
appear, although there appears to be at least one exception,
the *Shah Name* in prose composed for Abu Mansur, governor of Tus, mentioned above. Since all that is preserved of
that version is the preface, which is found attached to some

manuscripts of Firdosi's *Shah Name*, little can be said about the original complete work.

The Persian translation of Tabari's great Arabic chronicle was made by the *vezir* Abu 'Ali Muhammad Bal'ami at the order of Mansur b. Nuh. He started his work of translation in 963 and finished it several years later. The Persian version is more an adaptation than a translation of the Arabic original. As such it is important as an early example of New Persian style, not as a calque on the Arabic. The commentary, or *Tafsir,* on the Quran by the same Tabari was also translated from Arabic into Persian by a group of learned divines assembled at the order of the *amir* Mansur. The introduction to the Persian translation tells us that it was difficult for many persons to understand the Arabic original, so the *amir* convened the learned men of Transoxiana to issue a decree on the propriety of translating a commentary on the Quran into Persian. They agreed and even cited a verse from the Quran *(Sura* Ibrahim, 4) in support of translation. Then it was translated.

Several works on drugs and medicine, written in Persian during the later Samanid period, are of less interest since they were obviously greatly influenced by Arabic models. One of the texts, the *Hidayat al-muta'allimin* of Abu Bakr Akhavani Bukhari, composed in Samanid Bukhara, is of special interest because it contains words peculiar to the Persian dialect of Bukhara.

The decline of the 'Abbasid caliphate paralleled the development of local Arabic dialects in various parts of the Islamic world, emphasizing regional diversities. In the Iranian part of the Islamic world Classical Arabic continued in

use as a language of religion and science, but no more of
poetry, literature or communication. But New Persian more
and more usurped the role of Arabic in all fields, until by the
twelfth century very little Arabic was written in Iran or
Central Asia, except religion and science. Sometime during
the Samanid period, Persian became the language of bureaucracy and government, but the process of change is uncertain.
We do not have information in the sources, but I suggest
that the change was gradual. Probably Arabic was used for
diplomacy, or for occasions when elegance was required.
Otherwise Persian came to be written increasingly for internal matters, until by the end of the Samanid era it was
supreme. The oral means of communication was always
Persian if not a local Iranian dialect.

Just as earlier the provincial cities of the caliphate reflected the splendor of Baghdad, so under the Samanids,
their provincial towns followed Bukhara. On the northern
frontier the economic and commercial growth of Khwarazm
made this province especially receptive to foreign ideas, and
the incoming wealth enabled patrons to subsidize literature
and learning. Archaeology tells us that the number of towns
in Khwarazm increased in the tenth century, which is not
unexpected. The "academy of Ma'mun" named after the first
Khwarazmshah, who assumed the title in 995 after killing
his rival, became the center of cultural activity in the province. Under his son, the next ruler of Khwarazm, both al-
Biruni and Ibn Sina, the two great savants of the age, found
support in the academy.

The famous scholar and scientist al-Biruni (more properly

Beruni) was born in 973 in a village of southern Khwarazm. He studied mathematics, astronomy, medicine, and history and became a walking encyclopedia. He had a powerful, investigating mind which touched a myriad of disciplines and problems. He wrote a history of his own land, Khwarazm, which unfortunately has not survived save for a few excerpts in other works. He was a true and loyal son of Khwarazm, maintaining a patriotic feeling for the land and its rulers until the end of his life. His first work was a book called *Athar al-baqiyya,* or "The Surviving Remains" of old cultures and civilizations, which is a mine of information about various ancient customs, different calendars, and the like. Although he was a Sunni Muslim, he showed interest in and sympathy for several heretical movements. From his own writings it is clear that Gurganj, the capital of Khwarazm, had many savants and a long tradition of culture. After all, the great mathematician, Muhammad b. Musa al-Khwarazmi, came from that land, and it is from his own name that we derive the word algorism. Furthermore, the names of several astronomers are also known from pre-Biruni Khwarazm, and al-Biruni's teacher, Abu Nasr al-Mansur, was a prominent mathematician.

In 1017 Mahmud of Ghazna conquered Khwarazm and ended the local dynasty. As an important figure in the local court, al-Biruni was brought as a prisoner to Ghazna, where he was well treated and permitted to write. In this period, which lasted thirteen years, al-Biruni had the opportunity to study India and write his famous book on India, which was finished about 1031. He was able to return to his home-

land but found it devastated by Turkish nomads, so he returned to Ghazna, where he died in 1048 or in 1051, in the
reign of Maudud, grandson of Mahmud.

Many of al-Biruni's writings have survived, including a
book on mineralogy, several tracts on astronomy and geography, and a book on medicine or pharmacology. He was
known as the most learned man of his age, and showed
himself an exact scientist in many respects ahead of his time.
His measurement of the earth's radius was short by only
twelve miles, and other feats of trigonometry were equally
remarkable. He knew of the heliocentric theory of our solar
system, but he operated with the geocentric theory in his
own works on astronomy.

The correspondence between al-Biruni and Ibn Sina shows
that the former was a philosopher as well as a mathematician,
astronomer, etc., and in some respects a partisan of the views
of Rhazes in natural philosophy. Since al-Biruni had some
concept of fossils and the changes on land and sea in pre-
historic ages, he also held a philosophy of history of the
evolution of various civilizations. In his theory of the rise
and decline of a culture, culminating in a catastrophe and
then followed by a new prophet, he anticipated some modern
philosophers of history. Al-Biruni remains one of the most
remarkable intellects of history and an ornament of his land
and age.

A compatriot of al-Biruni was Muhammad b. Yusuf al-
Khwarazmi (died *ca.* 997), who probably served in the Samanid bureaucracy, since he wrote about it in his book
Mafatih al-'ulum, "Keys of the Sciences," a small encyclopedia of both the natural sciences and Islamic subjects such

1. Wall painting from Varakhsha

2. Statuette of a woman from Varakhsha

3. Old Bukhara street scence

4. Mosque of Magoki Attar

5. Close-up of mosque of Magoki Attar

6. Minareh Kalan (12th century)

7. Plaster (*gach*) prayer niche ca. 11th century

8. Metal mirror (Seljuk period)

9. Mausoleum of Samanids

10. Close-up of mausoleum of Samanids

11. Carved wooden architrave of mosque (12th century?)

12. Page of Qur'an, dated 361 A.H./971 A.D.

as jurisprudence, grammar, traditions, etc. From his work we may surmise that the Samanid court was interested in various branches of learning other than literature and religious subjects. There were philosophers, astronomers, and other savants in Nishapur, Samarqand, Merv, Balkh, and other cities of the Samanid kingdom, but one of them should be singled out, not because he came from Bukhara, but because his influence on Islamic thought was enormous. I refer to Ibn Sina or Avicenna, as he was called in the Latin West.

Ibn Sina was born at Afshana, a village near Bukhara, in 980. His father, originally from Balkh, was a functionary in the Samanid bureaucracy and also an Isma'ili in his religious sympathies. Ibn Sina was an infant prodigy who studied all the disciplines of his age and acquired a reputation for his great knowledge even as a youth. He studied and practiced medicine, and while still a boy he was able to cure the *amir* Nuh II b. Mansur of a disease which had baffled the court doctors. As a result, he was given permission to use the famous court library of the Samanids, which he described as a treasure house of knowledge. Shortly after he used the books, probably in 998, the great library was accidentally burned, a great loss for the Islamic world because it undoubtedly contained many unique manuscripts.

In 1001, after the fall of the Samanids, Ibn Sina's father died and his son was appointed to his father's position. In 1004 he fled to Khwarazm, where he met al-Biruni. Here he remained for at least five or six years until he left for western Iran. He had many adventures and lived in various cities such as Rayy, Hamadan, and Isfahan, until he died in 1037 at Hamadan, where his tomb exists to this day.

One recent bibliography of Ibn Sina's works listed 242 titles, the variety of which reveal the sage as an excellent example of the medieval universal man. Perhaps his most famous work was the *Shifa,* "Remedy," dealing with logic, physics, and metaphysics, really an interpretation of Aristotle. This book was first translated into Latin in the twelfth century and enjoyed great popularity in western Europe. Another of his important writings was the *Qanun fi'l-Tibb,* or "Canons of Medicine," which earned for its author the title of the second Galen. It too was early translated into Latin and for almost five centuries remained a required textbook in the medical faculties of western Europe. Ibn Sina was not only a compiler and classifier of knowledge, although he did this to an extraordinary degree, but he was the foremost Muslim philosopher who created a universal and consistent system of thought. In Europe, Avicenna (from the Spanish form of his name) was called the "philosopher of Being," inasmuch as he wrote so much about this. He based his observations on Aristotle and Plotinus, since for the Islamic world the two were mixed together, because of Neo-Platonic works purporting to be the writings of Aristotle.

This is not the place to discuss Ibn Sina's philosophy, with its distinction between essence and existence, self-necessary being, and being which is necessary by another. Such distinctions, and an explanation of the terminology, would far exceed the limits of our inquiry. Enough has been said to show that Samanid Bukhara contributed to the highest science and thought of the time. Both Ibn Sina and al-Biruni, and probably others too, were not content to derive all of their knowledge from the writings of their predecessors.

Both great scholars made personal observations and study of the sciences; for example Ibn Sina corrected several longitudes of cities, and al-Biruni's activity in astronomical observation is well known. The parallel between al-Biruni and Ibn Sina is fascinating, for both did not shun political life but were advisers to several rulers. Both were religious men but tolerant and liberal in their views. Both typified the best qualities of the age, and both were raised in the Samanid domains, two jewels in the crown of Samanid Bukhara, even though they passed most of their lives elsewhere.

Samanid Bukhara has come down in history as the center of the "New Persian renaissance" in literature and culture, but, as we have seen, it was more than that. It was also a center of science and learning in the eastern Islamic world, and it played not a small role in the internationalization of Islam as a religion and as a civilization. The tolerance and liberalism of the savants who lived in the Samanid domains, if not always the government, enabled various beliefs in the domain of religion to flourish. Furthermore the "accrediting" of non-Arab ideas, a non-Arabic language, and non-Arab customs and mores, as consistent with Islam, took place in the Samanid kingdom. The test between an Arab and non-Arab Islam was met in Transoxiana, and henceforth concepts of second-class Muslims, because they were not Arabs or did not know Arabic, were to fade and give way to the international and universal Islam which we know. Some may argue that this process was inevitable, and that the Arabs even before the tenth century were obliged to accept the equality of distant peoples, cultures and customs, as genuinely Islamic, but the first time it was brought to fruition and accomplished, was in tenth-century Khurasan and Transoxiana. The fusing of Iran and Islam was, I believe, the greatest accomplishment of the Samanids, for which they should be remembered. I suspect that some of the learned men who lived then did realize what was transpiring in their time and indicated this awareness in their writings.

Some centuries are particularly productive, such as the fifth century B.C. and the nineteenth A.D. The tenth century in eastern Iran was similar. Although Bukhara was condemned by several contemporary writers as a cesspool, where the poor suffered greatly and the rich lived on the sweat and servitude of the downtrodden, such has seemed to be the paradox of many brilliant civilizations throughout history. The shining achievements of great philosophers, poets and artists have too often drowned out the suffering cries of the masses, and one would be amiss if he painted a rosy picture without the shadows. Perhaps one should remember the dark side as well as the bright side, but then that is not on what human dreams and aspirations are built. If it were so perhaps the dreams would not materialize.

· 6 ·

Turkish Ascendancy

> To the Turks belongs the *imperium*,
> while to the Persians *magisterium* and
> to the Arabs *sacerdotium*.
>
> OLD TRADITION

TURKISH PEOPLES now occupy most of Transoxiana and they
have spread far to the west even beyond Constantinople, but
this was a process lasting several centuries. And it continues
even down to the present in Iran where the Turkish dialect
of Azerbaijan apparently is spreading at the expense of Persian. How did the Turkification of the Samanid domains
proceed?

The steppes of Central Asia over which nomadic tribes
wandered have been compared to the sea. The attack of one
tribe on another would start a chain reaction, and the neighboring tribes then would suffer. It was not that Central Asia
was heavily populated, but rather the tribes required huge
expanses of pasture land, and pressures of any encroaching
tribe were quickly felt.

Herodotus described the chain reaction of the movements
of Central Asian peoples when he tried to explain the migration of the Scythians into South Russia in the eighth and
seventh centuries B.C., while later migrations of a similar
nature were reported by other Classical authors. Various
theories have been proposed for the causes behind the mi-

grations of tribes in Central Asia, such as the dessication of
the grass lands, population explosions, and new technologies,
such as the invention of the stirrup. Some evidence for most
of these theories has been found, but surely the factors, about
which we have little or no information, were many and com-
plex. Peoples of the steppes did move, however, and their
impact on Transoxiana and especially the oasis of Bukhara
is our concern.

Turks were people speaking tongues in one of the branches
of the Altaic family of languages. The Turkic group of the
Altaic family was probably old and widespread in Siberia
and Central Asia even before the formation of the first Turkish steppe empire in the middle of the sixth century A.D. If
there were Turkic speaking nomads who accompanied various hordes invading the Near East or India before that
time, they left no record and we can only surmise that Turks
were to be found among the Hephtalites and perhaps other
Central Asian peoples who moved into the Near East in pre-
Islamic times. The formation of a Turkish Empire in Mongolia in 551 soon brought the Turks into Transoxiana. As
mentioned above, the Turks destroyed Hephtalite power
circa 565 and asserted their own authority over the Sogdians
as far as the Oxus River, which remained the boundary between the Sasanian Empire and the Turks. Although the
empire was divided into an eastern and a western kingdom
during the years 582–603, the Turks were to remain the
dominant power in all of Central Asia for over five centuries.

There were many different tribes of Turks, the names of
which we learn from various Arabic and Persian books, but
the most valuable of all is the *Divan Lughat al-Turk* or a

compendium of the Turkish languages by Mahmud of Kashgar who wrote his work in the eleventh century. There is much information about the Turkish tribes and their histories in the text under the Turkish word entries, whose explanations are given in Arabic. The political changes in the Turkish empires of the steppes cannot concern us here, but a brief survey of the situation at the beginning of Samanid rule, and changes in the tenth century would be of interest.

Perhaps the most important Turks in the history of the Near East were the Oghuz, who lived for the most part north of the Aral Sea. It is uncertain whether the word Oghuz originated as a political grouping of tribes, but it later seems to have had an ethnic sense, at least in the eyes of the Muslim authors. The Oghuz extended almost to Europe, where their western boundary was the Emba River, the eastern frontier of the Khazar Kingdom. Along the Syr Darya (ancient Jaxartes River) were many Oghuz settlements, trading centers where not only Turks but Sogdians and Khwarazmians also lived. Kashgari tells us that the inhabitants of the cities of Taraz, Isfijab, Balasagun, and others in the northern part of Transoxiana spoke Turkish and Sogdian. All had the dress and customs of the Turks, however, an indication of the Turkification of the populace. Most of the Turkish slaves in the time of the 'Abbasid caliphate came from the Oghuz.

The Arabs, in their conquests in Transoxiana, had to fight against the Turkish people called the Türgish, who lived in the northeast, Issyk Kul (Lake) region. About 766 the Türgish were replaced by the Qarluq, who in turn were subordinate to the Uighurs farther to the east in Mongolia and in Sinkiang or Chinese Turkistan. After the destruction of the Uighur steppe empire by the Qirgiz in 840, the Qarluq became the leading steppe power on the northeast frontiers of the growing Samanid domains. The Samanids extended their boundaries to the north and northeast at the expense of the Qarluq. Isma'il, the first Samanid, captured Taraz, one of the Qarluq capitals, but he and his successors had to repel Qarluq raids from Kashgar and elsewhere. In the early part of the tenth century, Muslim missionaries converted some of the Qarluq leaders to Islam, which meant a great change in the allegiances of the Turkish tribes. Henceforth the Turks were not outsiders, or stray converted slaves, but part of the Islamic world, and an important factor in later history.

A twelfth century author, Sharaf al-Zaman Tahir Marwazi, wrote the following regarding the Oghuz: "When they came in contact with the Islamic domain, some of them became Muslims and were called Türkmens. Hostilities occurred between them and the others who had not accepted Islam. Then the number of Muslims among [the Oghuz] increased, and the position of Islam among them became better. They conquered the infidels and drove them away. . . . The Türkmens spread throughout the land of Islam and improved their character there to such an extent that they ruled over most of the [Islamic domain], becoming kings and sultans." This would also apply to the Qarluqs and other Turks.

It is important to dispel the notion that Central Asia was divided between settled Iranians in Transoxiana and nomadic Turks to the north of the Syr Darya. We have men-

tioned the mixture of Sogdians and Turks, but even before
the Samanids, Turks were settled in towns in the Ferghana
valley and elsewhere in Transoxiana, while Turkish nomads
probably had displaced the Iranian-speaking nomads in the
steppe and desert areas by the time of the Arab conquests.
Soviet archaeological discoveries in Central Asia have confirmed the picture presented by written sources, that towns
existed in the areas ruled by Turks, inhabited both by Turks
and Iranians, while both settled and nomadic Turks were
also found in the Samanid Kingdom. As the number of
Turks increased, the Sogdians, Khwarazmians, and others
became assimilated, a process well advanced by the time of
the Mongol conquests at the beginning of the thirteenth
century.

Islam, then, broke the wall between Iran and Turan and
made a Turkistan of the lands north of the Oxus River. Probably most of the early Muslim missionaries to the pagan
Turks were unofficial religious mendicants, or dervishes, who
accompanied the Islamic *ghazis* in their expeditions against
the Turks, but who remained in non-Muslim lands to convert the pagans. Not all of the Turks were pagans, or followers of shamans, for Manichaeism, Christianity, and
Buddhism had many converts among them. The teachings of
Islam must have sounded familiar to many Turks. A passage
in the celebrated Arabic book called the *Fihrist* by Ibn al-
Nadim (died 995) tells us that a Uighur ruler in Chinese
Turkistan, who was a Manichaean, heard that the Samanid
amir (Nuh b. Nasr?) planned a persecution of the Manichaeans living in Samarqand. Whereupon the Uighur
(called Toquz Oghuz by Ibn al-Nadim) declared that there

were more Muslims in his domain than Manichaeans in the Samanid Kingdom, and if the Samanids persecuted the Manichaeans there, he would do the same for the Muslims in his land. This was enough to stop the Samanid *amir*.

According to tradition, a brother of *amir* Isma'il took refuge with the Turks in Kashgar and converted a prince of the ruling family to Islam. This ruling family became known to Arabic and Persian authors as the Ilik khans, or the Al-i Afrasiyab, and in European scholarship as the Qarakhanids. Great uncertainty about the Qarakhanids existed until O. Pritsak found the explanation of the shifting titles found in the sources (see bibliography). Briefly, the principle of "double kingship" existed among the Qara-khanids (as well as other Turks), whereby a fixed system of offices and titles applied to the ruling family. We cannot go into that system in detail, but the totem title Arslan "lion" was held by the co-ruler of the east or right branch of the Turks, while Bughra "camel" was the title of the west or left wing. There were also sub-rulers with their titles, Arslan Tigin, Yinal Tigin, and others. A man might move from a lower post to a higher post, and this practice confused the Islamic writers. After the conversion of the Qarakhanids to Islam, their Muslim names remained with them in spite of changes in titles, which makes their identification easier. It was through the Qarakhanids that East or Chinese Turkistan was opened to Islam.

The conversion to Islam of some Turks in Central Asia in the tenth century may reflect the general missionary efforts sponsored by the caliph and other Muslim rulers of the time. The embassy of Ibn Fadlan to the Volga Bulghars in 921 had political motivation, but the desire to spread the Sunni beliefs prevailing in Baghdad was also evident. Sam'ani, in his collection of biographies, the *Kitab al-Ansab,* tells of a certain Muslim preacher in the lands of the Qarakhanids called al-Kalamati from Nishapur, who died in 961. Other such missionaries are mentioned by Sam'ani and other sources, which indicates the continued activity of Muslim missionaries among the pagan Turks. Although we have no direct evidence for a concerted Muslim missionary effort organized by the governments, "non-official" *ghazis* were especially active under the Samanids, and the conversion of many Turks to Islam was the result.

Islam must have weighed lightly on the new converts, for we hear of shamanistic practices among the Central Asian Turks which lasted even down to the present day. Such beliefs in magic and sorcery did not prevent at least the Turkish leaders from adopting Sunni Islam, and indeed throughout later history the Turks strongly maintained their allegiance to Sunni Islam. Although the Central Asian Turks rarely followed Shi'ism or other heresies, in later times they did join mystical orders which were known as the dervish orders. Probably pre-Islamic practices and rites did survive in some Muslim dervish practices among the later Turks. So a new element was added to the Islamic cultural amalgam, beginning in the tenth century, but greatly increased in the eleventh and twelfth centuries.

Turks, of course, held special positions in Baghdad at the court of the caliphs, even before the time of the Samanids. Their military prowess and reliability are reported in the sources, and it was not unnatural that they should rise to important posts in Baghdad. The spread of Islam and mass conversions to Islam in Iranian lands made Central Asia and the Caucasus area the best sources of supply for slaves. Consequently, pagan Turkish slaves were much in demand in 'Abbasid Baghdad. Furthermore, slaves were not only secured by military expeditions; in times of peace they could be purchased. For the Turkish tribes in Central Asia frequently fought among themselves, and like the Negro tribes in West Africa in the eighteenth century, they sold their captured enemies to the Muslims, so a steady supply of slaves from Central Asia was provided for the caliphate.

Slaves were an important means of wealth and Turkish slaves were valued highly. 'Abdallah b. Tahir is reported to have sent the caliph a tribute consisting of two thousand Oghuz slaves among other items, including textiles, sheep, and horses. 'Amr b. Laith is reported to have trained slaves to serve as spies for him, and then he gave them as presents to his chiefs. The slave marts of Baghdad were especially active, for the highest prices for slaves could be secured in the capital. The Turkish slaves, in effect, replaced the free Arab warriors or *muqatila,* who had remained on the caliphal payrolls from the early Islamic period. To spend money on reliable slaves was much better than giving it to Arabs with uncertain allegiances.

The early Turkish slaves, in Baghdad for the most part, worked as domestic servants and as bodyguards. They showed themselves to be reliable and capable administrators as well as warriors, so it was not unexpected that the Turkish guards of the caliphs should acquire a special importance not just in military affairs but also in the administration of

affairs of state. The Turkish soldiery in Baghdad became
so disliked by the populace that the Caliph al-Mu'tasim in
836 moved the capital north to a new city called Samarra,
and from 836 to 892 the Caliph's court was there. Nine caliphs
lived there as puppets of the Turkish guard, who made and
unmade caliphs. The power and central authority of the
caliphate suffered, and similarly the provinces were not free
from Turkish officers. In 868 the Turkish governor of Egypt,
Ahmad b. Tulun, declared his independence and set up a
dynasty called in history the Tulunids.

Although our information about the provincial capitals is
much less than about Baghdad, we may assume that in the
matter of Turkish slaves, as in other respects, the provincial
centers copied Baghdad. It would seem, however, that neither
the Turks at the court nor those in the army were as yet prominent in Nishapur under the Tahirids. Isma'il had a large
number of *ghulams,* or young slaves in military service, but
they probably were not exclusively Turkish. Certainly Iranian *dihqans,* as well as Turks, served as officers in the Samanid army, in which all kinds of people were enrolled.
The Turkish *ghulams,* of course, were attached to the court
and not to a *divan* or bureaucratic apparatus of state. The
expeditions of Isma'il against Taraz and elsewhere in Turkish areas swelled the slave marts of Bukhara, and under
his son Ahmad we hear of many Turks in the royal guard.

Nizam al-Mulk, in his *Siyasat Name,* describes in detail
the ideal training of *ghulams,* perhaps best translated as
"pages," under the Samanids. According to the author, the
first year after a page was bought was spent in learning
obedience and discipline; in the second year he acquired a

horse and learned how to manage it. Every year he had new
duties and lessons to learn, such as the functions of a cup
bearer and a robe bearer. If the page were skillful and capable he could advance to the post of commander of a troop
or afterwards to that of chamberlain. The ultimate appointment was governor of a province, which gave a large measure
of independence. There is no evidence that there was a school
for pages which was organized on a systematic basis, but
even the unorganized training made of the Turkish slaves
competent leaders in the administration as well the army.

The "slave" army of the Samanids was modeled on the
Turkish army of the caliphs, as well as drawing from old Iranian
or Central Asian traditions." The Sasanian army, as
well as the military forces of local pre-Islamic rulers in
Transoxiana, was primarily composed of cavalry drawn from
the nobility, while the mass of foot soldiers and others who
accompanied the army were relatively unimportant. The
Iranian feudal lord and his retinue may have been models
for the caliph and his slaves, but the slave institution in
Islamic times had no forerunner, insofar as we can detect, in
Sasanian Iran. The slave soldiers of Islamic times were imported and were without local loyalties and families, which
gave them a special flexibility and strength. The system of
importing non-Muslim slaves and making a special guard
of them persisted throughout Islamic history, culminating
in the famous Janissaries of the Ottoman Empire.

There were, of course, many slaves other than Turks, such
as Indians, Slavs, Armenians, Greeks, and Africans, any non-
Muslims being eligible. Somehow it was easier for all but
the Turks to become absorbed into what might be called the

Islamic melting pot. The Turks, however, maintained their identity. This observation was made as early as the beginning of the ninth century by the encyclopedist al-Jahiz. Certainly history favored the Turks and they made good use of their opportunities, whereas Indian, African, and other slaves remained slaves and never formed distinct groups. The principle of a slave army became so fixed in Islam that later when the Caliph al-Muqtafi (1136–1160) dispensed with his Turkish slave guard, he had to recruit Greeks and Armenians in their place.

The Turkish military slaves then came to form a special category of slaves called pages, and this is the institution with which we are concerned. It was, in fact, the concept which secured rule for the Turks and established the tradition later in the Islamic world that the Turks were meant to be soldiers and rulers, whereas the Persians were relegated to the arts, crafts, manners, and literature, all of which were called *adab* in Arabic. The Arabs specialized in religion.

The government, of course, tried to control the slave trade, more to secure profits than from any humanitarian motives. There were customs duties on imported slaves and a frontier control point could be very profitable for its master, so the caliph farmed out such posts to the highest bidders. The transit trade in slaves through the Samanid domains was regulated by that government, which issued licenses for the purpose. The economic importance of the Turkish slave trade was emphasized by several Islamic authors, and one geographer of the tenth century, Ibn Hauqal, claimed that some Turkish girl and boy slaves were sold for as much at 3,000 gold *dinars* a person, which was a fortune for the time.

At first the Turkish soldiers of the Samanid rulers kept to their profession of warfare, for under the early *amirs* of the dynasty there was sufficient activity on the frontiers of Transoxiana, in Khurasan, Seistan, and elsewhere to keep the army occupied. When a slave soldier was killed or died, his property went to his superior officer or to the ruler. Turkish officers and especially generals, however, began to acquire lands and other possessions, hence became interested in the welfare of their families and friends. One of the early Samanid generals, Qaratigin (died 929), refused to buy or accept as a present any landed estates, since they would change his purely military capacity and would restrict his actions. He was exceptional, however, and other Turkish generals were not slow to amass wealth of all kinds.

The number of pages at the Samanid court was several thousand, but many more slave soldiers served in the army. We have little information about the Samanid army, but much more about their successors, the Ghaznavids. Bosworth (see bibliography) has assembled data about the latter army which give a basis of comparison for the Samanids. The most striking feature of Mahmud of Ghazna's army was the multiplicity of peoples and races in it. Indians, mountaineer Afghans, Iranians, and even Arabs served beside the Turks. This multiplicity was praised by later authors, who saw in the various contingents the means by which a ruler might play one group against another and thus prevent intrigues and combinations. The Samanid army was surely less varied, but there are indications that at times there was a division into groups, each seeking its own advantage at the expense of the others. The situation, however, was much more complicated than an initial glance at the linguistic picture might imply. From the linguistic-cultural milieu, one might expect three groups in the Samanid capital of Bukhara: the Turks, the aristocratic Iranian *dihqan* class with their attendants speaking Persian, and the masses speaking Sogdian dialects. But Islam had leveled these apparent barriers. Thus a more realistic description of the "solidarity groups" with influence on the exercise of power, would consist of the military class, comprising both Turks and Iranians; the bureaucracy, which had influence but no troops; and the masses, with power based on the possession of weapons, who were led by religious leaders.

It seems to me that the creation of a professional military caste of Turkish guards under the Samanids was more the desire of the ruler to find a pendant against the masses than his wish to subdue the Iranian *dihqans,* as often has been stated. When Isma'il first came to Bukhara, the power of the local mob and of brigands in the oasis frightened him. One must not forget that at this period in Transoxiana the populace was generally armed, and, once united, became a powerful force. Furthermore, it was not only, or not so much, the local populace which was a problem for the ruler, but rather the continuous influx of volunteer warriors for the faith, the *ghazis,* which created many problems for the government. The *ghazis* in the Samanid domains are mentioned many times in the sources, for the frontier against the pagan Turks was a popular refuge area for all kinds of people from the Islamic world. Just as on the frontier against the Byzantines and Armenians in the west, so to Transoxiana came religious heretics fleeing persecution, soldiers of fortune,

brigands, and others for various reasons. By the last half of
the tenth century, however, the conversions to Islam of so
many Turks ended the frontier, and the *ghazis* left the
Samanid domains for other fields.

We know about the migrations of large groups of *ghazis*
from Transoxiana to the west and south. The wars of the
Ghaznavids in India attracted many *ghazis* to the south,
which we learn from many sources. Likewise such authors
as Ibn al-Athir and Ibn Miskawaih are full of information
about bands of *ghazis* from Khurasan passing through Boyid
domains on the way to the Byzantine frontier. For example,
in 966 a force of twenty thousand *ghazis* from Khurasan
appeared in Rayy, but they caused so much trouble by their
plundering that the Boyid prince Rukn al-Daulah led an
army against them, defeated them and sent them fleeing
back to Khurasan. The Boyids thought that this advance
of a *ghazi* band on the way to the Byzantine frontier was
in reality a Samanid plot to cause trouble for the Boyids.
The importance of the *ghazis* everywhere in the Iranian
Islamic world is indicated by the presence in many cities and
towns of an official known as the chief *(salar)* of the *ghazis*.

In the sources we find various names for the *ghazis*, such
as *'ayyar, sa'luk, fityan, muttawi'a,* and it is difficult to determine just what the distinction was between them. Ya'qub
b. Laith rose from one of these groups in Seistan, and such
people continued to flourish in the province under the Samanids. Indeed one might compare the eastern Islamic world
with the American West during the nineteenth century,
when local bands of vigilantes were formed to provide security and law for the towns and settlers. Sometimes the dis-

tinctions between a robber band of *'ayyars,* a group of *ghazis,* and a fraternity of *fityan* resembling dervishes were blurred and indistinct, but the very proliferation of such groups indicates the unsettled conditions of life and the need for local organizations of defense.

As long as the central government was strong and could keep the *ghazis* under control there was a minimum of fragmentation of authority, but with the decline of the Samanid state, loyalties shifted and various local forces came to the fore. The "military establishment," if we may so term it, lost its initial spirit as the defender of orthodox Sunni Islam and instrument of the propagation of the faith against the pagan Turks. The Turkish generals became more concerned with carving out private domains for themselves in the Samanid Kingdom. This was an imitation of the previous policy of the *dihqans,* whose properties now were being taken over by military leaders. Force of arms provided the justification for the military usurpation of civil prerogatives. The acquisition of estates by generals was the beginning in eastern Iran of the *iqta'* system which became so popular under later dynasties, especially the Seljuks.

The problem of the rise of the *iqta'* system has not been resolved satisfactorily in spite of much research on the subject. One, if not the main, difficulty is the confusion of terminology in the sources, for anything related to taxes and money or land tenure is liable to be complicated. It is not the place here to investigate the background of land owning and taxation problems in Islamic history, but any attempt to understand the situation in the oasis of Bukhara will, unavoidably, call upon parallels elsewhere for information.

Since the *iqta'* system appeared in full bloom under the Qarakhanid successors of the Samanids, we should look to see whether it or its forerunners existed under the Samanids.

We should go a little into detail regarding the meaning and use of the word *iqta'*. The word originally meant a portion of state land given to someone to manage in return for taxes, service, or various other conditions. These conditions, for which state lands were leased, varied considerably, and are strictly speaking not a defining part of the *iqta'*. Obviously, in this wide usage *iqta'* existed from the beginning of Islam, but we cannot be concerned with early uses here. The practice of renting or leasing state lands for tax farming and for other reasons, existed under the *'Abbasids*. On the whole under the early *'Abbasids* both civil and military officials received salaries in cash, although payment in slaves, produce and even land was not unknown.

When we come down to the Boyids, the frequent union of civil and military offices in one person, and the payment for past and future military service to that person by assigning him to an *iqta'*, led to changes in the meaning of the word, which was further developed under the Seljüks. Frequently the person to whom an *iqta'* was assigned did not live on the land but sent his representatives to collect revenue from the peasants, which was his payment for past and future service to the state. Gradually, under the later Seljüks, the holder of an *iqta'* came to exercise all of the functions of the state on his lands. The resultant breakdown of central authority was not unexpected, but this too is beyond our concern. Did this system, which is generally described as a fief system, develop in the late Samanid period as it seems to have done in the late Boyid era?

The early Samanids had the means to pay the army in money or movable property, not only because they controlled the extensive silver mines of the upper Zarafshan River, but more because of the flourishing trade and prosperity of their kingdom. There was no reason for the *amirs* to make land grants of state lands; indeed the early rulers strove to buy land, as we learn from our sources. With the economic difficulties in the second half of the tenth century, the clamor of the army and the royal guards, who had taken over real control of the bureaucracy, for more rewards grew. Almost half of the Samanid budget went to the army, and the demands of the soldiery were still not filled. There is no evidence, however, that the central government actually gave lands as *iqta'*, even though the Samanid bureaucrat al-Khwarazmi defines the word in his book as land given by a ruler to a person who obtains the revenue from it, which would indicate at least a knowledge of the wider usage of the term. The point in question, however, is not the word or general practice of granting land as payment for services, but the recognized institution, which combined civil and military authority in a "fief," to be held as long as the recipient rendered military service. This institution was not flourishing under the Samanids, if it was at all practiced. This did not mean that generals did not buy land or acquire estates as gifts, but they owned them and did not hold land in a special feudal relationship to the *amir*. Indeed the Turkish general Alptigin is supposed to have owned five hundred villages, plus villas, caravansarais, many sheep, horses, etc. Since most of the histories dealing with the Samanids also relate the circumstances leading to the rise of the Ghaznavids beginning with Alptigin, it may not be amiss to describe his rise to power.

Alptigin was a Turkish *ghulam* who had risen to the rank of captain *(hajib)* of the royal guard by the time of the accession of the *amir* 'Abd al-Malik b. Nuh in 954. Under the new *amir* the power and influence of Alptigin and other Turkish generals greatly increased. In 961 he was appointed governor and commander of the army of Khurasan but he did not hold this office long because the death of 'Abd al-Malik and the coming to the throne of Mansur b. Nuh changed his position, depriving him of his former influence at court. Following the lead of another general Qaratigin, who had earlier carved out a principality for himself from his governorship of the town of Bust in southern Afghanistan, Alptigin abandoned his extensive lands and property in Khurasan and Transoxiana and moved into the mountains of Afghanistan. With a small force of personal slaves and followers he conquered Ghazna and established a principality. He died in 963 and was succeeded by his son, who made peace with the Samanids and nominally accepted their suzerainty. After his death in 966 the Turkish troops in Ghazna elected Bilgetigin, who had been a slave of Alptigin, to be their head. Bilgetigin governed Ghazna for the Samanids and made raids into India, where he obtained much booty. After his death in 975 there was a short rule of another of Alptigin's *ghulams* until in 977 he was deposed and Sebüktigin, still another of Alptigin's slaves, became the ruler of Ghazna. Under Sebüktigin the raids on India were increased and the principality of Ghazna, though nominally a governorship of the Samanid Kingdom, grew in size at the expense of its neighbors.

We do not know what contractual arrangements or vassal status existed between the central government in Bukhara and local dynasties such as the Hindu kings of Kabul, the rulers of Chaghaniyan, the two princes of northern and southern Khwarazm, and others. They acknowledged Samanid hegemony, sent tribute or gifts, and provided military support for Bukhara, but it would seem that local authority and practices were maintained with a minimum of direction from Bukhara. The provincial governorships, however, were under the direct control of Bukhara, and the most important, as well as the most extensive, was that of Khurasan. There was a dichotomy of the Samanid domains, the lands north of the Oxus River being ruled from Bukhara and those south of the River from Nishapur.

We are fortunate in having considerable information about Nishapur, both in local histories in Arabic and Persian and in ample descriptions of the city by the geographers. If Nishapur can be taken as a model for the other large cities of the Samanid realm, then certain overall observations about the kingdom can be made. If the "vassal" states, such as Khwarazm, Chaghaniyan and Isfijab, are excepted, then the areas ruled directly from Bukhara were restricted to a relatively small area. Alptigin went to Nishapur as governor of the province and commander of the army of Khurasan; how did he manage affairs?

Nishapur, as well as other cities such as Herat, Merv, and Tus, had a mayor or *ra'is* who was usually a member of an important local family, although outsiders could be sent from Bukhara to the city. In Nishapur the mayor came from the prominent Mikali family, and the office practically became hereditary, although a nominal appointment came from Bukhara. The city of Nishapur and surrounding districts then was really governed by the Mikalis. This does not mean that the Mikalis were always unopposed, for there were rival groups in the city. According to the geographer al-Maqdisi, most cities in Khurasan and Transoxiana had several factions, divided by social factors, conflicting commercial interests, or simple geography, in different quarters of the town. Samarqand, Merv, and several smaller towns are singled out by him as having factions especially addicted to violent disputes. In Nishapur, the "upper city" to the west competed with the rest of the city, but, as in other cities of Iran, purely social antagonisms were complicated by religious factors, in this case opposition between Shi'ites and Karamites, followers of Ibn Karram. Bukhara, however, was more free of internal conflict in this period simply because the central governmental authority was there. After the fall of the Samanids, the situation changed and the religious leaders of the city had to assume political control.

The leaders of the populace of Bukhara were the Hanafite judges and learned men, and one name among them stands out in the early part of the Samanid period, the previously mentioned family of a certain Abu Hafs. The relationships of various persons of this family are confusing in the sources, but we learn that the first prominent man of the family Abu Hafs al-Kabir (d. 832) had been a student of the Hanafite scholar Muhammad b. Husain al-Shaibani (d. 804) in Baghdad before returning to Bukhara. He became the leading Hanafite authority in Bukhara and wielded much influence not only among his colleagues but over the masses. His tomb was on a hill near Bukhara bearing his name, and it became a place of pilgrimage. His son Abu 'Abdallah b. Abu Hafs was the person who wrote to Nasr b. Ahmad b. Asad, the Samanid *amir* of Samarqand, requesting from him a ruler for Bukhara. Abu 'Abdallah came out of the city to meet Isma'il, Nasr's brother, when he approached Bukhara in 874, and he fully supported Isma'il until his death in 877. Another Abu 'Abdallah b. Hafs is mentioned as the chief of the *ghazis* of Bukhara in the time of the *amir* Nuh b. Mansur, who held him in high esteem, but his relationship to the family of the Hanafite judges is unknown. We know that after the decline of Qarakhanid power the Hanafite judges called the Al-i Burhan took over rule of the city. So the situation in Bukhara was not quite the same as in other cities of the Samanid domain.

Not only were the judges responsible for legal affairs but they were also teachers. There is no evidence that organized colleges, like the later Nizamiyya college of Baghdad, existed in Bukhara in the late Samanid period, and any notices in the sources about *medresas,* as they were later called, are anachronistic. In those days teachers gave lessons in their own homes or in a *ribat,* which is best translated as "cloister" or "fortified mosque." On the Islamic frontier, *ribats* were forts where *ghazis* gathered to fight the nomads or infidel Turks, but as the frontier receded the word *ribat* changed its significance to become a synonym for mosque or religious school. It is interesting to note that the word was brought to the Volga Bulghars and appears in old Russian chronicles as *ropat,* meaning a Muslim mosque. Whereas the term *medresa* was not used in the Samanid period, it does appear shortly after the fall of the Samanids, and it was certainly imported into Baghdad from the east. Consequently one may conjecture that the incipient institution did exist at the end of the Samanid period. A *medresa* would be defined as a higher school where several professors taught various subjects in some sort of a program. The sources fail us and we cannot determine whether there were such schools in Bukhara or other cities of the Samanid Kingdom, but if they did exist at the end of the dynasty they were probably recent innovations.

If one were to collect the names of the *'ulama,* or learned men in religion, who flourished in Bukhara, from various sources, the list would be impressively long. As we have mentioned in the case of Ibn Sina, the fame of Bukhara as a center of learning lasted till the very end of the Samanid dynasty and beyond. Certainly Bukhara continued as a center of the arts and crafts, but we have few definite remains from this period. Strangely, none of the buildings of the Samanids, save the so-called tomb of Isma'il already mentioned, have survived, whereas from the Qarakhanid period and later there is much. One may suppose that some Samanid structures were rebuilt in later periods, but the extensive use of wood, so prone to destruction by fire, probably accounts for the absence of early buildings lasting down to today.

What happened to the well-organized government and bureaucracy built by Isma'il and his immediate successors? We read in the sources about Isma'il's accomplishments, which must have been many in spite of the tendency of writers to attribute to the founder of a dynasty many later achievements or virtues. Isma'il, for example, was credited with standardizing the weights and measures in his kingdom, and some weights have been found inscribed with his name, indicating the veracity of the written sources. On the other hand, much of the state structure must have evolved over a period of time rather than being all a creation of the first *amir* of the dynasty. The bureaucracy, as far as can be determined, continued to expand, as bureaucracies usually do, but the main change in later Samanid times was that the bureaucracy became completely subordinate to the military leaders. Nuh b. Nasr had to conciliate the guards to ascend the throne, while succeeding princes held their power by virtue of support by the military, and they realized this full well by rewarding and bribing the generals. Nonetheless, the government structure created by the Samanids was respected even by the Turks, and it aroused admiration in the eyes of later writers. Furthermore, it was the model for the later dynasties of Ghaznavids and Seljüks.

When the ruler was strong, he held the power groups of his realm together, but, as we have mentioned, when the ruler was weak the military party dominated the government. The generals, however, did not usurp positions in the bureaucracy but rather worked through puppets in the bureaucracy. The divisions between the three classes of influential people in the Samanid state were rather strictly maintained. One might almost characterize the three classes as castes, a continuation of the ideal tripartite society of pre-Islamic Iran: the priests, warriors, and scribes above the

masses. In the Samanid state then, the three "institutions" of
power and influence were the army, headed by the commander of the army; the bureaucracy, headed by the prime
minister; and the religious leaders, headed by the chief of
the Hanafite judges. The last also might be described as the
judicial branch of the government, but apparently more and
more the religious leaders thought of themselves as apart
from the government, until at the end they refused to encourage resistance to the Qarakhanids on the grounds that
they were above the power struggle. The bureaucracy, however, became a pliant civil service maintaining certain customs and standards, but willing to take orders from any
victor in the struggle for power. So the *amir* and his army
remained the instrument of executive power in the kingdom.
The slave army was better than a purely mercenary army
which could be hired, for the slaves did maintain some
loyalty towards their masters. But the solid basis for co-
operation among all groups, laid by Isma'il, had vanished
by the end of the tenth century. Henceforth the key word
in Islamic theories of statecraft was not co-operation, but
balancing of one party against another; and the ruler in order
to survive would have to show great skill in playing off powerful groups or factions against each other. This, I believe,
is one of the prime reasons for the fall of the Samanids.

That the bureaucracy and military were considered quite
distinct, and not open from one to another, even at the top
levels of the Samanid state, is indicated by the distribution
of titles, or better termed honoraria (Arabic *laqab*), by the
amir. Theoretically, the caliph alone should issue honorary
titles, but the ruler of Bukhara, as representative of the

caliph, also assumed this prerogative. The Samanid rulers themselves did not take many titles, and during their lifetimes they were normally called by their patronymics *(kunya);* thus Isma'il was addressed as Abu Ibrahim by his associates. After death, the rulers were referred to by epithets such as *al-shahid,* "the martyr," applied to Ahmad b. Isma'il, and *al-sadid,* "the just," given to Mansur b. Nuh. On the coins of the Samanid rulers, however, we sometimes find *laqabs,* such as *al-malik al-mu'ayyad,* "the king assisted (by God)" and others. It should be noted that the title *maula amir al-mu'minin,* "client of the commander of the faithful (the caliph)," also appears on some Samanid coins showing the *de jure* dependence of the Samanids on Baghdad. Nizam al-Mulk and other later authors praise the Samanids for their simplicity and unpretensiousness, which was in marked contrast to the flattering hyperboles assumed as titles by later rulers.

The later Samanid rulers did give *laqabs* to their Turkish generals and others in positions of authority. Nizam al-Mulk has a chapter on the subject of titles, part of which deserves to be quoted in some detail. He writes:

> Titles must suit the persons who hold them. Judges, imams and scholars have had titles like Majd ad-Din [Glory of the Faith], Sharaf al-Islam [Honor of Islam], Saif as-Sunna [Sword of the Ordinance], Zain ash-Shari'a [Ornament of the Religious Law], and Fakhr al-'Ulama [Pride of Scholars]; because scholars are concerned with "the religious law" and "the faith." If anyone who is not a scholar takes these titles upon himself, not only the king but all men of discretion and learning should refuse to countenance it,

and that person should be punished so that everyone observes his station. Likewise the titles of army commanders, *amirs,* assignees, and commissioners have been distinguished by the word *daulah* [empire], for instance, Saif ad-Daulah [Sabre of the Empire], Husam ad-Daulah [Sword of the Empire], Zahir ad-Daulah [Protector of the Empire], Jamal ad-Daulah [Grace of the Empire] and suchlike; while civil governors, tax collectors, and officials have been given titles with the word *mulk* [kingdom], like 'Amid al-Mulk [Pillar of the Kingdom], Nizam al-Mulk [Harmony of the Kingdom], Jamal al-Mulk [Grace of the Kingdom], Sharaf al-Mulk [Honor of the Kingdom], and so on. It was never the rule that Turkish *amirs* should take upon themselves the titles proper to civil dignitaries or vice versa. But after the time of The Fortunate Sultan Alp Arslan (may Allah have mercy upon him) customs changed, discretion disappeared and titles became mixed up; the smallest person demanded the biggest title and was given it, with the result that titles became cheap.

Nizam al-Mulk further complains that in his day the proper order of titles was ignored, such that titles appropriate for scholars were given to soldiers, and the system became a mockery. He says:

> The extraordinary thing is this, that the most insignificant Turkish students or pages, as irreligious as can be, who have committed a thousand crimes and wrongs against religion and state, give themselves the titles of Mu'in ad-Din [Supporter of the Faith] and Taj ad-Din [Crown of the Faith].

So the government of the Samanids, which had been so highly praised by contemporary authors, and in retrospect

136

by later writers, was not the same at the end of the dynasty as at the beginning. The same elements were present; perhaps the machinery of state was much improved and even more efficient, but the spirit was different and the men were different. Perhaps it followed the course of certain laws of history, or possibly the Samanid state became the victim of changing times, but one thing is significant that ever after, in this part of the world, Iranians lost the rule to the Turks. When Isma'il ascended the throne, Iranians not only were ruling but they were pushing forward the frontier of Islam at the expense of the Turks. At the end of the dynasty, the Iranians had retreated to the schools and *divans* of the civil service. This was a great change in world history and deserves to be noted.

· 7 ·
the fall of the Samanids

Bukhara is like the cadaver of the world.
ABU MANSUR 'ABDUNI

To FOLLOW the sequence leading to the fall of the Samanid
dynasty is difficult because of the host of personages involved, further complicated, as we saw in the last chapter,
by the proliferation of titles, such that sometimes in the
sources we do not know whether "the *amir*" means the
Samanid ruler or a Turkish general. Mansur b. Nuh died
in 976, the year the Samanids lost control of the silver mines
on the upper Zarafshan River, and his son Abu'l-Qasim Nuh
ascended the throne as a minor.

The new *vezir* 'Abdallah b. Ahmad al-'Utbi fortunately
proved to be a capable administrator, and at first his attempts
to restore influence to the bureaucracy at the expense of the
military were successful. The powerful governor of Khurasan, as well as the commander of its army, Abu'l-Hasan
Simjuri, was given titles and privileges until he felt himself
secure, but then in 982 he was deposed. He was a member
of a family which had served the Samanids well for many
years. The Simjuris had acquired extensive lands in Kohistan
south of Herat, as well as elsewhere, which they managed
like a feudal appanage. The Simjuri family by no means
vanished but continued to flourish even after the fall of the
Samanid dynasty.

Abu'l-Hasan Simjuri retired to his own estates, and a
Turkish general, who was closer to the prime minister,
Abu'l-'Abbas Tash took his place in Khurasan. The military
energies of the realm were mostly directed against the
Boyids, for the northern frontiers were no longer the borders
between the realm of Islam and that of the infidels. So the
Boyids became the chief enemies of the Samanids.

The Boyids were the most successful of several dynasties
which ruled in western Iran in the tenth century. All of these
dynasties were Shi'ite, but the Ziyarids, the descendants of a
certain ruler of Gilan called Mardavij, belonged to a Shi'ite
sect called Zaydis, the followers of which had spread Islam
in many parts of the Caspian provinces. The Zaydis followed one of the Shi'ite leaders or *imams,* called Zayd instead
of his brother Ja'far al-Sadiq and his progeny, to whom other
Shi'ites gave their allegiance. When Mardavij extended his
sway over western Iran in the early part of the tenth century, he had many Daylamites from Daylam, the highlands
and mountain areas of the Caspian provinces, with his army,
among them three brothers of the Boyid family. The brothers, however, did not remain with Mardavij, for they began
to carve out principalities of their own. After Mardavij was
murdered in 935, the Boyid brothers inherited most of his
realm and much more. The eldest, 'Ali, ruled the province
of Fars, al-Hasan ruled al-Jibal, or the Isfahan-Hamadan
area, while Ahmad acquired Kirman and then Khuzistan.
In 945 Ahmad conquered Baghdad, and shortly afterwards
the caliph bestowed on the brothers the titles by which they
are known in history, 'Imad al-Daulah ('Ali), Rukn al-
Daulah (al-Hasan), and Mu'izz al-Daulah (Ahmad).

The Boyids were at the height of their power in the second half of the tenth century. When 'Imad al-Daulah died without a son, his brother Rukn al-Daulah sent his son 'Adud al-Daulah to rule Fars, and when in 977 his father died, 'Adud al-Daulah became the head of the family and the real ruler of all Boyid domains. He proved a formidable foe of the Samanids.

Some scholars have emphasized the difference in religion between the Samanids and the Boyids, and have attributed much of the hostility to this. The Ziyarids, who were also Shi'ites, became allies, or even vassals, of the Samanids in the common action against the Boyids. The latter, although partial to the "twelver" Shi'ites, the same branch which is dominant in Iran today, also accepted Zaydis and Isma'ilis into their ranks, as well as Sunnis. So religion seems a poor excuse for the hostilities between the two sides. Furthermore, the Boyids later fought the Fatimid caliphs, who were Isma'ilis, in Syria and northern Iraq, hardly a sign of Shi'ite solidarity. It is true that the Samanids rejected the Caliph Muti' raised by the Boyids in place of al-Mustakfi, but hardly out of any sympathy for the latter.

It was rather the foreign policies of the Samanids and Boyids that almost inevitably brought the two into conflict. The Boyids continually fought the Ziyarids, who first sought Samanid help, and then, in repayment for the aid, recognized the suzerainty of Bukhara. It was only natural for the Boyids to exploit any weakness of their opponents, hence any rebels against Samanid authority, such as the Simjurids, were sure to receive help from the Boyids.

In 982 Tash, the new governor of Khurasan, led an army

to aid Qabus, the Ziyarid, and other local Caspian princes, who had been dispossessed by the Boyid armies. At first successful, the Samanid army was then put to rout and fled back to Nishapur. Earlier the Samanids had lost Kirman to the Boyids, although Samanid rule there had never been secure. 'Adud al-Daulah defeated the nomadic Baluchis and other tribes of Kirman, extending Boyid rule to hitherto isolated areas and even to pagan districts. The death of 'Adud al-Daulah in the following year probably saved Khurasan from a Boyid invasion. Gurgan, the country to the southeast of the Caspian Sea, however, remained under Boyid rule until Qabus eventually returned there in 998, but that was at the end of Samanid rule in the East.

The Samanids, although they were the great rivals of the Boyids, were no longer powerful enough to stem the disintegration of their own kingdom. Internal troubles multiplied, as became increasingly clear, and these more than anything else brought about the fall of the dynasty. Human factors, of course, were important, and not only were the last members of the dynasty weak but their ministers and advisers were not distinguished. To many contemporaries, the course of history seemed to predict the imminent fall of the dynasty.

Although Abu'l-Qasim Nuh b. Mansur (977–997) was a patron of scholars and poets, he did not have the power or strength of character to really rule, and consequently he became a puppet in the hands of one party or another. The party of Tash and the *vezir* al-'Utbi opposed Abu'l-Hasan Simjuri and the chamberlain called Faiq. The prime minister, al-'Utbi, however, was murdered in 982 by some pages instigated by Faiq. Tash, who was still commanding the Samanid army of Khurasan in Nishapur, made preparations to attack Faiq and the Simjuris, Abu'l-Hasan and his son Abu 'Ali. Peace was made, however, and Faiq was given Balkh to rule, Abu'l-Hasan, Qohistan, and his son Abu 'Ali, Herat, while Tash kept Nishapur. This arrangement did not last long since Tash's friend al-'Utbi was dead and the new *vezir,* who had been an enemy of al-'Utbi, was also hostile to Tash. The prime minister, Muhammad b. 'Uzair, persuaded the *amir* Nuh to remove Tash and reinstate Abu'l-Hasan Simjuri as governor of Khurasan. Tash did not give up but requested help from a Boyid prince whom he had aided when the latter was with him in exile. Even with the troops sent from Rayy by the Boyid, Fakhr al-Daulah, Tash was defeated by Abu'l-Hasan and had to flee to the Boyid realm, where Fakhr al-Daulah gave him the district of Gurgan to rule as his lieutenant. Tash remained in this capacity until his death early in 988. The Simjuris were now the most powerful group in the Samanid kingdom.

Abu'l-Hasan died in 988 and his office was given to his son Abu 'Ali Simjuri, although the *amir* seemingly did this only out of fear of Abu 'Ali. Faiq saw his chance and became reconciled with Nuh. Hostilities broke out between Faiq and Abu 'Ali, but the former was defeated in 991 and consequently Abu 'Ali was granted some of the domain of Faiq to rule. Faiq retreated toward Bukhara but was again defeated by Bektuzun, a general of Nuh's, and fled to Balkh where he was able to maintain himself. Such was the situation when the Qarakhanids intervened.

The sources disagree as to who invited Bughra Khan to

attack Bukhara; according to the historian Abu Nasr Muhammad al-'Utbi in his *Kitab al-Yamini,* it was primarily Faiq and some others. Gardizi does not speak of any invitation, while Mirkhond and other later historians claim that Abu 'Ali invited the khan to divide the Samanid domains between them. Ibn al-Athir and others say many Samanid generals and officials wrote to the khan asking him to come. In any case he came and was successful.

The advance of the Qarakhanids was by no means swift or unexpected. We have already mentioned the loss of the silver mines on the upper Zarafshan River in 976, but it is uncertain whether the Qarakhanids took them or some local rulers did. The western ruler of the Qarakhanids, Bughra Khan, known also by his Muslim name of Harun al-Hasan b. Sulaiman, conquered Isfijab, north of present Tashkent, in 980. That district had been ruled by a minor Turkish dynasty under the Samanid overlordship. We do not know of further encroachments on Samanid domains, but one may assume that there were losses of territory. The stage was well set for a conquest.

Bughra Khan, it was claimed, was further incited to the conquest of Transoxiana by a certain Abu Muhammad al-Wathiqi, a descendant of the 'Abbasid caliph Wathiq, according to al-Tha'alibi, who claimed that this religious leader had great influence on the khan. The *amir* Nuh sent an army against Bughra Khan, but it was defeated and the commander taken captive. In desperation Nuh turned to the erstwhile rebel Faiq, made him governor of Samarqand, and sent him troops to defend the district against the Qarakhanid leader. The course of events is not clear, but Faiq surrendered to Bughra Khan, possibly after some fighting. Faiq was sent by the khan to Balkh as his vassal. Nuh fled from Bukhara and the Qarakhanids entered the city at the end of May, 992.

Nuh did not go far, only to the town of Amul on the Oxus River, where he wrote to Abu 'Ali Simjuri exhorting him to come to the aid of the house of Saman, but Abu 'Ali refused. Fortunately for Nuh, help was not needed, for Bughra Khan became ill in Bukhara and decided to evacuate the city and return to Turkistan. In July he departed, leaving a certain 'Abd al-'Aziz as his deputy. It is possible that certain Türkmens attacked the khan's army after he left Bukhara, but the sources are uncertain. On the way back to his home Bughra Khan died, and Nuh returned to Bukhara in August, easily defeating the khan's deputy.

Faiq, however, attempted to reassert his authority in Bukhara, but was defeated by Nuh and fled to Abu 'Ali. The two rebels determined to put an end to Nuh's reign, but the *amir* found another supporter. Nuh turned to Sebüktigin of Ghazna for aid. Sebüktigin joined forces with Nuh, who also was able to secure the aid of the ruler of Khwarazm and others. In August, 994, Sebüktigin defeated Abu 'Ali and Faiq who fled to Fakhr al-Daulah, the Boyid ruler of Rayy. After the victory, Nuh bestowed on Sebüktigin the title of Nasir al-Daulah and on his son Mahmud the title of Saif al-Daulah, and Mahmud was named governor of Khurasan in place of Abu 'Ali Simjuri.

In 995 Faiq and Abu 'Ali learned that Nuh had returned to Bukhara and that Sebüktigin had gone to Herat, leaving Mahmud in Nishapur. In a surprise attack, the two forced Mahmud to evacuate the capital of Khurasan. The two then sought a reconciliation with Nuh, probably hoping to separate him from Sebüktigin. They were unsuccessful and there was another battle near Tus in July, 995, which ended in defeat for Faiq and Abu 'Ali. This time they fled towards Khwarazm and again sought pardon from Nuh. Nuh was willing to forgive Abu 'Ali but not Faiq. Events in Khwarazm, however, changed the picture.

Khwarazm was divided into two parts, the southern ruled by a dynasty of Khwarazmshahs, and the northern part ruled by the *amir* of Gurganj or Jurjaniyah, at this time called Ma'mun b. Muhammad. At this time Ma'mun attacked the Khwarazmshah and captured him and his prisoner Abu 'Ali. The latter he sent to Bukhara, where he was reconciled for a time with Nuh, but then at the request of Sebüktigin, Nuh turned him over to the ruler of Ghazna in 996. The latter kept Abu 'Ali a prisoner for over a year and then executed him.

Faiq had fled to Nasr Khan, the Qarakhanid successor of Bughra Khan, where he intrigued to incite him against Nuh. Nasr Khan, however, made peace with Nuh and Sebüktigin, as a result of which Faiq was not only pardoned but made governor of Samarqand by Nuh. Sebüktigin remained the ruler of all provinces south of the Amu Darya, while the Qarahkanids controlled much of the land to the north of the river. In the year 997, not only did both Nuh and Sebüktigin die, but also Fakhr al-Daulah and Ma'mun, who had become the sole ruler of all of Khwarazm.

Nuh was succeeded by his son Abu'l-Harith Mansur, who was still a boy. Quarrels with his advisers led to a request for intervention in the affairs of Bukhara to Nasr Khan from some of the ministers of Mansur. The Qarakhanid came to Samarqand and sent his ally Faiq towards Bukhara. Mansur left the city, but Faiq professed friendship, so the *amir* returned; but it soon became apparent that Faiq was the real master of affairs.

At the death of his father, Mahmud was involved in a struggle for the throne of Ghazna with his brother Isma'il. Consequently he left Khurasan, and *amir* Mansur appointed the Turkish general Bektuzun to the post in Nishapur. When Faiq came to Bukhara he incited Abu'l-Qasim Simjuri, brother of Abu 'Ali, to return from Rayy, where he had been with the Boyids. A struggle between Bektuzun and Abu'l-Qasim ended in victory for the former, but peace was made and Bektuzun retained Nishapur while Abu'l-Qasim assumed the rule of Herat and Qohistan. Mahmud, after securing the throne of Ghazna, returned to Khurasan to reoccupy the post of governor, which he had vacated. He captured Nishapur and Bektuzun fled to Bukhara.

Faiq and Bektuzun united forces and decided to remove Mansur. They deposed and blinded the *amir* in February 999, raising his younger brother 'Abd al-Malik to the throne. Mahmud of Ghazna thereupon threw off all allegiance to the house of Saman, and in the Friday prayers substituted the name of Qadir, the 'Abbasid caliph, for that of the Samanid *amir*. Mahmud defeated Faiq and Bektuzun in Merv at the end of April 999. After obtaining the submission of the local rulers of Chaghaniyan and Gharchistan, Mahmud appointed his brother Nasr governor of Khurasan. The center of power had shifted from Bukhara to Ghazna.

Faiq was preparing a new expedition against Mahmud

146

when he died. The Qarakhanid khan decided to put an end to Samanid rule and moved towards Bukhara in the autumn of 999. The attempts of the Samanid government to rouse the people of Bukhara against the Qarakhanids has been described by an eyewitness, recorded in a book of history by a certain Hilal al-Sabi, and it deserves to be recorded here.

"I was," he said, "in Bukhara at the time of the arrival of the Khan's armies. The Samanid preachers ascended the Mosque pulpits and called on the people to enlist, saying in the name of the Samanids: 'You are aware how well we have conducted ourselves and how cordial have been the relations between us. This enemy now menaces us, and it is your manifest duty to help us and fight on our behalf. So ask God's grace in succouring our cause.' Now most of the people of Bukhara as also of Transoxiana are bearers of arms. When the common people heard this they consulted the jurists on the subject of fighting. The jurists dissuaded them, saying: 'If the Khan's followers were at variance with you on religion, it would be a duty to fight them. But where the object of dispute is temporal, no Muslim has a right to risk his life and expose himself to bloodshed. These persons [*i.e.*, the enemy] are well-conducted, and orthodox: it is better to keep away from the fray.' This was one of the chief causes of the victory of the Khanites, of the rout of the Samanids, and the extinction of their empire. The Khanites entered Bukhara, conducted themselves well, and dealt kindly with the populace."

So the Muslim Turks accomplished what the pagan Turks could not have done—the conquest of the Samanid kingdom. There is little evidence that the Shi'ites or other heretics welcomed the Qarakhanids, while the Sunnis upheld the regime. Rather it seemed as though the Samanids had lost support from all of the people, regardless of their religious sentiments. In his advance to Bukhara, the khan declared that he was a friend of the Samanids, and the Samanid military leaders, such as Bektuzun, voluntarily surrendered to the invaders. The Samanid *amir,* however, was arrested with many members of his family and sent in captivity to Turkistan.

There is an adventurous sequel to the fall of the Samanid dynasty. A younger brother of Mansur b. Nuh, and of 'Abd al-Malik, the last Samanid *amir,* called Abu Ibrahim Isma'il, escaped from his imprisonment in Turkistan and made his way back to Bukhara, where he remained hidden for a time. Then he went to Khwarazm, where he assumed the name Muntasir and proclaimed a revolt against the Qarakhanids. His forces were successful in defeating and driving the troops of the Qarakhanids from Bukhara and then from Samarqand. At the very turn of the millennium it seemed as though the star of the Samanids was again rising, but it was only for a very short time. At the approach of the main army of the Qarakhanids, Muntasir, as he is known in the sources, evacuated Bukhara and went to Khurasan. There he fought with Nasr, the brother of Mahmud of Ghazna, defeating him, and forcing him to retreat from Nishapur to Herat.

The defeat of Nasr occurred in February, 1001, but it was far from decisive. Mahmud came with reinforcements to aid his brother, forcing Muntasir to flee to Boyid territory. Muntasir returned shortly, and after a temporary occupation of Nishapur, was decisively defeated and fled to Transoxiana in 1003. There he made an alliance with the Oghuz Turks, who were moving into the areas north of the Amu Darya. With their aid he was able to defeat the Qarakhanids again, including the chief khan himself. The Oghuz tribesmen, however, were unreliable and Muntasir did not want to depend on them for support, so he left them and fled south. Then he tried to reconcile Mahmud of Ghazna by writing to him about the past associations of the Ghaznavids with the house of Saman, seeking to rouse Mahmud's sympathy. This attempt failed, however, and Muntasir tried his luck again in recrossing the Amu Darya to enlist support in Transoxiana. He gathered troops, including a detachment of *ghazis* from Samarqand as well as some Oghuz tribesmen. In May, 1004, he succeeded again in defeating the Qarakhanid army. The khan, however, returned with new forces and completely routed the Samanid forces, capturing many leaders of the army. Muntasir again fled to Khurasan, but new hope of support brought him back still another time to the oasis of Bukhara.

The last attempt to gain power proved to be a debacle, for the small forces he had with him abandoned Muntasir, and finally his camp was surrounded and his brother and chief supporters were captured. Muntasir managed somehow to escape. The would-be *amir* took refuge with an Arab tribe in the vicinity of Merv, but there he was killed by them in 1005, according to some sources by order of the Ghaznavid governor of the district. Thus ended the last hope of the Samanids, and, although members of the family continued to live in the oasis of Bukhara, they never aspired to leadership. The age of the Samanids was over.

The Samanids were defeated by superior force, but the circumstances leading to the fall of the last Iranian dynasty of Central Asia should be examined, and then the consequences may be assessed. To turn first to the military side, a careful survey of the sources reveals an inherent weakness in all of the armies or military establishments of this period. Whereas at the beginning of the tenth century a popular army composed of various elements of the people was not unusual, by the end of the same century the professional army was everywhere dominant. The popular wars against the infidel Turks in Central Asia came to an end. A crusade against internal heretics would rouse only half-hearted support, since heresy was no longer a threat to the Islamic community, now universal and without danger from internal pagan foes. The vast majority of the population of both Iran and Transoxiana by the year 1000 was Muslim, at least in practice, even though many may have been inclined to views at variance with the tenets of Sunni orthodoxy.

We have already mentioned the exodus of the *ghazis* from the Samanid domains, heading south to India or west to the Byzantine frontier. This migration eliminated a popular power factor, leaving the military establishment virtually unopposed in the Samanid state. Since the religious leaders and the populace no longer had the military force to assert themselves, they were obliged to resort to passivity, with a consequent withdrawal from involvement in the politics of the various parties in the kingdom. The conquest of Nishapur by one leader and its recapture by another, for example, did not mean that the populace of the city was in one instance victorious and in another defeated. Rather it meant that one leader with his Turkish slaves and mercenary army took over the direction of the government and bureaucracy while another leader with his slaves and mercenary army left the city. Neither one nor the other leader expected much help from the people of the city. Acquiescence in the change of authority, with a willingness to pay taxes and any special levies to the new rulers, was the most that was expected of the populace. With this attitude prevalent among the masses there is no wonder that the key to success was not popularity among the people, but rather a strong, professional army and adequate funds to pay them.

The professional army, led by Turkish slave generals, had replaced the old "feudal" levies, whereby the *dihqans,* or landed nobility, had led their followers, and even peasants, to join the ruler of the state, be it the Sasanian king of kings or the ruler of the oasis of Bukhara. The mercenary army was certainly more efficient than the nondescript forces of previous days. It would seem, on the other hand, that Transoxiana in the tenth century was exceptional among the lands of Islam, in that the population as a whole bore arms. This was probably a continuation of the time when conditions in the frontier province required every inhabitant to be on guard against raids of the nomads. By the eleventh century, however, Transoxiana was well on the way to becoming a Turkistan, and the situation had changed.

Archaeological evidence indicates that Arnold Toynbee's challenge-and-response theory of history applies well to the Bukharan oasis in the tenth century. The great walls around the oasis represent the response to the challenge of invasion by nomads. Land was irrigated and cultivated up to the walls and even beyond. The policy of the Samanids to abandon the great walls in favor of a forward policy against the steppes, proved successful not only in spreading Islam, but also in containing the nomads. Apparently it also had some negative results, one of which was the relaxing of efforts in the oasis of Bukhara to hold back nature as well as man. Economic factors, which we shall examine below, were undoubtedly of prime importance in the abandonment of the land, but the encroachment of the desert on the oasis was the end-result of the official policies and political developments. We cannot be sure of the rate of decline, but by the time of the Mongol conquest in the early thirteenth century all of Central Asia had declined in comparison to what it was in the tenth century.

The decline of Central Asia is not only seen in the oasis of Bukhara but elsewhere, and most vividly in the city oases of Chinese Turkistan or Sinkiang. There the encroachment of the sands of the desert on irrigated fields and settlements has been revealed by archaeological expeditions. Towns buried in the sands of the desert give evidence of the power of nature as well as the negligence or the inability of man to cope with his manifold problems. From written records, as well as archaeology, it would seem that the tenth century in Chinese Turkistan too was a century of prosperity and flourishing civilization followed by a decline. Let us delve further into the social and economic reasons for the decline.

From the sources we know that in the oasis of Bukhara land values, which were very high during the reign of Isma'il, tumbled at the end of Samanid rule. The translator of Narshakhi's book into Persian says that in his time (*circa*

1128) the estates near the city of Bukhara, called "the villas of the Magians," were given to whoever wanted them free of charge, since the burden of taxation and other problems made of them a liability rather than an asset. This situation was paralleled elsewhere, and gives further evidence of an economic crisis in the eleventh century, which is generally known as the great shortage of silver.

An analysis of extant Samanid coins shows that early in the tenth century the silver content was of high quality, while at the end of the same century we find alloys of silver, which continue to deteriorate in the percentage and quality of silver with the post-Samanid coins of the eleventh century. The great shortage of silver in the Muslim world from the end of the tenth to the middle of the thirteenth century has been noted by many writers, who, for the most part, have attributed this important fact solely to political factors, such as the expansion of the Turks, the fall of the Khazar kingdom in South Russia, and general political instability in the Muslim world. Our examination of the political conditions in cities, the centers of trade and commerce, would lead us to suspect that more basic economic factors lie behind the silver shortage, although the results of political instability certainly contributed greatly to the process.

As long as the state as well as trade was flourishing, the Samanid practice of a double currency seems to have worked well. There was an internal and an external coinage, the former limited to several areas in Transoxiana and the latter to external trade and international transactions. The various coins of the "Bukhar Khudah" type, mentioned above, were used in the oasis of Bukhara, Shash, and elsewhere,

whereas the normal Islamic silver *dirhems,* with Arabic
formulae but no figure on them, were exported to Russia
and to the west of the Islamic world. It was not profitable to
export the "Bukhar Khudah" coins together with the regular Islamic *dirhems* because the rate of exchange of the
former in Bukhara was higher than that of *dirhems.* Furthermore, the people of eastern Europe wanted good silver and
would not accept alloyed coins. With the decline of the
Samanid state, so did the rate of exchange of the "Bukhar
Khudah" coins decline also, and the amount of lead and
other base metals in them was increased. The temptation to
debase the currency was strong when the Samanid ruler
needed more money to pay troops and to maintain the
swollen court. Economic consequences of the debasement
of coinage were not slow in appearing.

The important Samanid mints were in Samarqand, Shash,
and Andarab in the Hindu Kush mountains, thus all being
near silver mines. Bukhara, the capital, was also, of course, a
mint center. Undoubtedly there was a decline in the production of silver at the end of the Samanid dynasty, but other
factors too must have created the "silver crisis" of the eleventh
century. Political events, the drainage of silver to the west
by the Seljüks and other causes need to be studied. At present,
the disappearance of silver from the Muslim east has not
been satisfactorily explained. The raids of the Varangians
and the expansion of the Kievan state probably disrupted
trade between Transoxiana and eastern Europe, but again
details are lacking.

The great number of Samanid coins found in silver hoards
of the Viking Age in Russia, the Baltic area, and in Sweden

has fascinated many students. The early hoards, dated before 960 A.D., are composed almost exclusively of Islamic coins, while after that date Byzantine, German, and Anglo-Saxon coins appear beside the Oriental ones. At the end of the tenth century, the hoards cease and one assumes that the sole reason for this was that the line of communications with Central Asia was severed. Soviet numismatists and historians of medieval Russia, however, have shown that the Oriental *dirhems* were used as currency in Russia, for many halves and quarters of the coins have been found, and the Slavs might have continued using these coins if a new influx of western European coins had not started at the end of the tenth century. While we cannot go into this problem, it may be suggested that the internal silver crisis in the Samanid domains, plus a new orientation in the trade and economy of eastern Europe, together may have played major roles in the economic decline of the eastern Islamic world.

There seems to have been a general falling of the standard of living in the latter part of the tenth century. For example, al-Maqdisi, the geographer, writing in this period, decries the miserable earnings of the people of Merv, the dole, and the unhappy state of the common folk, which matters were not so well known elsewhere as the clothes, food, and baths of the city. The condition of the masses hardly can have improved as a result of the greater need for revenues on the part of the government, which we learn from the sources. The problems connected with water rights on the land are so numerous and complicated that we cannot deal with them here. Again, it would seem that conflicts over water, together with a possible sinking of the water table in the oasis of

Bukhara, brought economic hardships to the cultivators of land. We have already mentioned the spread of sandy areas at the expense of cultivation in the oasis. In Merv, according to al-Maqdisi, most of the water of the river which flowed to the oasis went on the state lands. The information we have, scant though it is, points to an impoverishment of the land and people upon it. This led to famines, most of them local, to be sure, but nonetheless terrible in their toll. The general situation in the eleventh century, however, must have made the tenth century seem like a golden age in comparison, for later the Oghuz bands and 'ayyars, or bandits, were especially destructive in orchards and cultivated fields. The cutting of trees, as we learn in the sources, was notably harmful, and we can imagine the consequences of deforestation.

Several times the decline of the *dihqans* has been mentioned as being part of the economic disorder we find in the eleventh century. Enough evidence exists to trace the decline of the *dihqan* class all over Iran as well as in Transoxiana. It is, of course, easier to trace the process over a number of centuries, and the situation at the beginning of the tenth century was quite different from that, say, at the end of the fourteenth. In 900 in Transoxiana, old, aristocratic Iranian *dihqan* families lived in their castles on their lands, and the estates were managed under an unconditional land tenure. The change from such unconditional to conditional land tenure (the *iqta'* system), caused the decline of the *dihqans* and their eventual disappearance as a class. By the fourteenth century, the military Mongol-Turkish aristocracy in the summer lived with their tribes, or their followers, as nomads in summer pastures, while in the winter they lived

156

at the courts of the rulers. The Iranian aristocracy, such as it was, on the contrary, lived in cities, and some families were known for their ancient lineage as *dihqans*. The word itself for a while came to be an honorary title before it sank to what it is today, a farmer or peasant.

Most of the Iranian *dihqans* easily changed masters and continued to serve new Turkish rulers, and some of them even became holders of *iqta'* lands under the Qarakhanids. The great majority of such *iqtadars,* however, were Turkish generals or even tribal chiefs who served the ruler. It must be emphasized again that the conquest of Transoxiana by the Qarakhanids was not just a military conquest but opened that area of Central Asia to Turkish colonization. Many Turks were attracted from the steppes to the south and set-tled down in the oases. Others came in nomadic tribal groups and occupied the pasture lands of Transoxiana. The process of the Turkification of Transoxiana continued for a number of centuries after the fall of the Samanids. Peoples mixed, and the pattern of social life under the Qarakhanids became complicated. Indeed the system of *iqta'* itself was by no means systematized or uniform, and the various forms of land ownership can be surmised only tentatively.

If we assemble information from all over the eastern Is-lamic world of the period from the fall of the Samanids to the Mongol conquest, at least six kinds of land ownership may be reported. First, we find *mulk* land (or Arabic plural *amlak*), which was land owned privately by either large or small landowners who paid taxes on it to the state and who could do what they wished with the land. The owners could sell it, add to *mulk* land, leave it to their children, or leave it as a trust *(waqf)*. Similar to privately owned lands were the special lands of the ruler *(amlak-i khass)*, which he could also sell or give away like his private lands. State lands *(divani)*, on the other hand, could not be treated as private land and could be sold, given as *iqta'*, or in *waqf* only under certain but varying conditions. All the income from state lands went into the state treasury, and this category of land was probably the largest of the six in the period which we are discussing.

Endowed (i.e. *waqf)* land was usually given to maintain a mosque, a school, or a hospital, and only later did endowments for private persons or families proliferate. For example, it seems that in Bukhara down to 1920 there was a quarter of the city where the descendants of the Samanids lived, supported by income from *waqfs*. Documents for such endowments are as frequent as the parish records of medieval England. Endowed land had to conform to the terms of the *waqf* and could not be sold or given away.

Feudal land or *iqta'* already has been mentioned. Legally, such lands could not be bought or sold by the *iqtadar* and were re-assigned at the death of the holder of an *iqta'*, or such lands returned to the category of state *(divani)* lands. In practice, however, all sorts of innovations existed. Finally there was a small category of land called community land *(jama'at)*, which belonged to the village, including surrounding orchards and pastures. Needless to say, the various modes of assessing and collecting taxes also were manifold, and the general picture of post-Samanid landholding and taxation is one of great complexity compared with the earlier period.

The change in the cities is not as noticeable since the general type of later Islamic city was being formed in the Samanid era.

Although we cannot determine the dates with any exactitude, one may say that the cities of the Samanid period differed from those of earlier eras, primarily in shifts in the centers of activity. Older towns were more or less restricted to the citadels with surrounding living quarters, or *shahristan,* enclosed with a wall. The great development of craft industries, trade and bazaars, especially in the tenth century, meant a shift of population to the suburbs or *rabads.* The security felt under the Samanid state, and the ending of any danger from attacks by infidel nomads, fostered a continued growth of the suburbs of cities in Khurasan and Transoxiana. As the cities grew, the gulf between the peasant and the urbanite also increased. The city dweller became more removed from the land than his predecessors of earlier centuries, and he also became more specialized in his work.

Unfortunately, the study of the internal organization of cities in Khurasan and Transoxiana has hardly begun and our sources about the social life of the city folk are scant. We do have evidence of various specializations in finished goods from city to city and this surely raised standards of workmanship. Just as the art of writing was a restricted profession open to those who were chosen by the scribes to enter their guild, so did the shoemakers, silver workers, and others organize themselves into craft guilds. In Bukhara, as in other cities of the eastern Islamic world, the guilds developed religious associations and later became associated with dervish orders. I believe the foundations for this development were laid in the Samanid period, although the sources refer only to later times.

It would be somewhat speculative to connect directly the development of guilds with the *ghazis* or with the Sufi or dervish orders, because we do not have enough information about them. It is true, nonetheless, that there seem to have been many associations or groups of people held together by mutual interests in the cities of the eastern Islamic world. Some guilds from the start probably had religious overtones, just as some of the Sufi brotherhoods had all kinds of people as members. The most famous example of a craftsman, who was also a *ghazi,* was, of course, Ya'qub b. Laith, founder of the Saffarid dynasty, and one may assume that there were many others. The organization of the *ghazis* is sometimes described in the sources as *futuwa* which word has been translated by some scholars as "chivalry," meaning an ideal as well as an institution. It is not surprising that volunteers for the holy war against infidels should have adopted rules for ascetic behavior or for a mystical life, which then became institutionalized. One might conjecture that after the wars for the faith ended in Central Asia, the organizations continued to flourish, even if in a changed manner, in the cities. This may have provided ties between the *ghazis* and craft guilds.

Bukhara at the end of Samanid rule was probably not much different from other cities of Khurasan, and various solidarity groups were flourishing there, some better organized and stronger than others. There is no evidence, however, that they occupied different parts of the city separated by walls. Although a number of quarters did exist in Bukhara, as we learn from Narshakhi and the geographers, there do not seem to have existed separate walls within the city, since the very walls of the houses and walled garden enclosures set off a maze of narrow streets which could hardly be called public thoroughfares. We may suspect that such groups as the Shi'ites in Bukhara tended to live close to each other, and possibly one quarter was favored by them as opposed to others. But our information does not permit more than reasonable hypotheses about the social structure of Bukhara, and they may change if archaeology brings new data to the contrary.

We hear about famines but very little about pestilence, plagues, and the sicknesses which were deadly in the Middle Ages in Europe. Inasmuch as Samanid Bukhara was crowded and dirty, and sanitation was a problem, epidemics must have decimated the population from time to time. The aristocracy and wealthy people could leave the city during an epidemic and take refuge in their villas in the countryside, but the poor folk had nowhere to go. There were doctors, of course, of whom Ibn Sina was the most famous, but real hospitals were a later development in the Islamic world. Garbage continued to be thrown into the streets, or more properly alleys, and the passer-by had to shout his coming to avoid being inadvertently hit from an upper window. City life in the Muslim world in this period may have been interesting but it was hardly easy for the vast majority of the population.

Bukhara lost its pre-eminent position as a capital after the fall of the Samanids. What changes were entailed in the transfer of authority from the Samanid *amir* to a lieutenant of the Qarakhanid supreme ruler? We must first look at the division of the Samanid domains between the Qarakhanids and the Ghaznavids, and then at the situation in Bukhara itself.

When Mahmud of Ghazna took over the rule of Khurasan it was not from the *amir* of Bukhara, who had long since lost control of the lands south of the Oxus River, but from independent rulers. Mahmud did not need to support his claim to the province by referring to the grant of the governorship of Khurasan to his father by the *amir* Nuh b. Mansur, for his military power could bring him sufficient legality for rule. Likewise, with or without invitations from some *dihqans,* or from others, the Qarakhanids had the power to occupy the lands north of the river. But neither Mahmud nor the Qarakhanids could control their own people, the Turks, who migrated in considerable numbers into Transoxiana and Khurasan. Ibn al-Athir, a historian of the time of the Mongol invasions, tells of the ravages of the Oghuz Turks, not only in Khurasan, but as far as Iraq and Anatolia, in the years shortly after the turn of the millennium. The most famous of these Turks, of course, were the Seljüks but there were many other bands ranging far and wide. For example, by 1038 the Oghuz were ruling in Hamadan, and in 1040 a Turkish band captured and plundered the city of Mosul in northern Iraq. The Ghaznavids, then, inherited much more than an empire; they found many problems, including the agents of their own downfall—the Turkish nomads.

The Qarakhanids, too, did not have a quiet rule in Transoxiana. Because of the policy of family rather than individual rule, internal politics within the Qarakhanid dynasty not only caused complications for the historian, but also for the dynasty, which was greatly weakened. Abu Nasr Ahmad b. ʿAli became the great *kagan,* or chief of the family ruling in Balasagun, after the death of his father in 998. The co-ruler of the western part of the kingdom was his brother Nasr b. ʿAli, also called Arslan Ilik, who ruled in the town of Özkend. This latter khan was the ruler who conquered Bukhara in 999, taking all of the Samanid princes back to his capital as captives. He left one lieutenant, Jaʿfar, or Chagri Tigin, in Bukhara and another in Samarqand. It seemed as though the Qarakhanids had become the heirs of all the Samanid lands north of the Oxus River and the Ghaznavids to the south, especially when a treaty between Nasr b. ʿAli and Mahmud established their boundary. Mahmud married a daughter of Nasr b. ʿAli in 1001 to seal the treaty.

Nasr, however, broke the treaty when Mahmud was busy in India and invaded Khurasan, where at first he met with little opposition. Mahmud returned and defeated Nasr, who then turned to his co-ruler of the eastern part of the Qarakhanid domain, Yusuf b. Harun, called Qadir Khan in the sources, a member of another branch of the royal family. Qadir was at that time spreading Islam in Khotan and elsewhere in Sinkiang, at the same time increasing his own power. A new army was assembled and again invaded Khurasan. The Qarakhanids were again defeated near Balkh in 1008, and this catastrophe led to internal conflicts among the members of the two branches of the family.

We cannot follow the internal strife of the Qarakhanids,

but Nasr b. 'Ali ruled the oasis of Bukhara, as well as other
areas of Transoxiana, until his death in 1013. He was followed by another brother Mansur b. 'Ali, who succeeded in
securing the office of chief *kagan* in 1015 or 1016. About the
same time we find a certain al-Husain b. Mansur ruling over
Bukhara, and although there is no sure evidence, we may
regard him as the son of Mansur b. 'Ali. This son of Mansur,
however, was under the jurisdiction of his uncle Muhammad b. 'Ali, who had moved into the position of his brother
Mansur when the latter claimed to be great *kagan*. Meanwhile peace reigned between Mahmud of Ghazna and the
Qarakhanids.

Mahmud of Ghazna, however, crossed the Oxus in 1017
and conquered Khwarazm. The Qarakhanids patched up
their quarrels long enough to send a united army against
Mahmud, but they were again defeated in 1019 or 1020.
This defeat broke the alliance and engendered new troubles
in the Qarakhanid domains. Another prince appeared on the
scene, a certain 'Ali Tigin, or 'Ali b. al-Hasan, possibly the
son of the Harun or al-Hasan b. Sulaiman, the Bughra Khan
who conquered Bukhara in 992. This 'Ali Tigin was a member of the collateral Kashgar-Khotan branch of the Qarakhanid ruling family. Pritsak has reconstructed the history
of 'Ali Tigin, who, it would seem, ruled in Bukhara some
time before 1015, when he was ousted by Muhammad b.
'Ali and al-Husain b. Mansur, as mentioned above. This
reconstruction is based on the coinage. 'Ali Tigin returned
to Bukhara in 1020, and with the help of the Seljüks, under
Isra'il or Arslan b. Seljük, he was able to defeat an army of

Muhammad b. 'Ali. 'Ali Tigin continued to rule Bukhara until his death in 1034.

The complexity of the titulary of the Qarakhanids confused outsiders, so the literary sources naturally reflect this. We are dealing with three phenomena, the Muslim name of the ruler, his Turkish title of rank, Bughra, Arslan, etc. mentioned above, and finally his Islamic *laqab* or honorary title. The last should have been personal; for example, Mahmud of Ghazna received the *laqab* "Yamin al-Daulah" from the caliph in Baghdad, and he is usually known by this *laqab* in the Arabic and Persian histories. The Qarakhanids, however, seem to have equated the Arabic *laqabs* with their own Turkish titles, for they usually did not receive them as honoraria from the caliph. Thus the coins from Bukhara from 1021 to 1025 carry the legend Baha al-Daulah Yagan Tigin, which must have applied to 'Ali Tigin. After 1025 he changed the Turkish part of the title to Arslan Ilik, which meant an increase in his power. He now ruled Samarqand and more, as well as Bukhara.

Mahmud of Ghazna again mixed in Qarakhanid affairs and crossed the Oxus. Yusuf Qadir Khan had become supreme *kagan*, but 'Ali Tigin and his brother Ahmad b. al-Hasan refused to recognize him as the supreme ruler, and Ahmad b. al-Hasan instead proclaimed himself as the great *kagan*. The latter seized Balasagun as well as Özkend, so Yusuf Qadir Khan turned to Mahmud for help. Mahmud and Yusuf Qadir Khan then made an alliance plus intermarriages of their children. Shortly afterwards Mahmud defeated the Seljük allies of 'Ali Tigin and took Isra'il a prisoner in 1025. 'Ali Tigin fled into the steppes but lost his wife and daughter as captives of the Ghaznavids. Mahmud, however, soon left Transoxiana and 'Ali Tigin returned to Bukhara. His brother Ahmad, however, lost to Yusuf and submitted to his authority whereas 'Ali Tigin did not.

The power of 'Ali Tigin continued to grow until Mas'ud, son and successor of Mahmud, sent an army, led by his vassal the ruler of Khwarazm, against 'Ali Tigin. The Seljüks again supported 'Ali Tigin, who won a victory over the Ghaznavids and Khwarazmians in 1032. Two years later 'Ali Tigin died and was succeeded by his son Yusuf b. 'Ali. Yusuf opened hostilities against Mas'ud, but then he broke with his old allies the Seljüks, who, after an uprising, first went to Khwarazm but then left for Khurasan. Yusuf, having lost his former allies, then made peace with Mas'ud the Ghaznavid.

Another Qarakhanid prince, Ibrahim b. Nasr, also called Böri Tigin, from the other branch of the Qarakhanids, in 1041 conquered Bukhara. This event, however, happened less than a year after the decisive defeat of Mas'ud of Ghazna by the Seljüks in the famous battle of Dandanqan, which ended Ghaznavid pretensions to rule Khurasan. A new era in the history of the eastern Islamic world had begun.

After the battle of Dandanqan in May, 1040, near Merv, the leader of the Seljüks, Toghrul, proclaimed himself ruler of Khurasan, with many titles, while Mas'ud gave up all pretensions to rule in Khurasan. The Ghaznavid sultan died early in 1041 and his successors retreated to Ghazna and directed their attention to India. The end of Ghaznavid rule in Khurasan in a real sense signified the end of the 'Abbasid-

Samanid system of government and rule in the eastern Islamic world, for the Ghaznavids were the last monarchs who attempted to restore the caliphal traditions of state. As such they were really the continuation of the Samanids. By caliphal traditions of rule, I mean the system under which the bases of power and wealth were primarily the state lands subject to taxes *(kharaj)*, plus a highly centralized bureaucracy. An interesting example of the attempt of Mahmud to bolster the centralization of his authority and to fight the tendency to give land in *iqta'* is provided by the *Siyasat Name* of Nizam al-Mulk, in speaking of Khwarazm.

> I heard that the amir Altun Tash . . . was appointed to be Khwarazmshah, and was sent to Khwarazm. Now the estimate of the revenue of Khwarazm was 60,000 dinars; while the salaries of Altun Tash's troops amounted to 120,000 dinars. A year after Altun Tash went to Khwarazm a person was sent to demand the revenue. Altun Tash sent his own emissaries to Ghazna and requested that the 60,000 dinars which were the burden [of taxation] of Khwarazm should be assigned direct to him for the payment of his troops instead of the money being sent from the *divan*. The *vezir* when he read this letter wrote an answer at once as follows, 'In the name of Allah The Merciful, The Clement; be aware that Altun Tash cannot be Mahmud in any respect. Let him take the money which he has collected in taxes and bring it to the sultan's treasury; having had the gold assayed and weighed, let him deliver it and take a receipt. Only then let him ask for the salaries for himself and his troops, and he will be given drafts upon Bust and Seistan; he will then send persons to go and collect the money and bring it to Khwarazm. Thus will be maintained the difference be-

tween master and slave, between Mahmud and Altun Tash, because the functions of the king and the responsibilities of the army will be clear and distinct.

Mahmud, however, was upholding a dying cause, and his frequent removal of powerful officials, with the confiscation of all of their property, did not halt the course of the fragmentation of central authority. With the coming to power of the Seljüks, the *iqta'* system was greatly extended, until it became dominant in the lands where the Turks held sway. The history of the Seljüks, of course, is bound up with Baghdad, Anatolia, and the Crusades. The crucial dates in general Islamic history are December, 1055, when Toghrul entered Baghdad, putting an end to Boyid power, and 1071, when his son Alp Arslan won the battle of Malazkird, capturing the Byzantine emperor Romanus Diogenes and opening all of Asia Minor to Turkish invasion. For us, concerned with Bukhara and Transoxiana, the Seljüks meant an extension to the west of influences current in Central Asia. Although the Seljüks invaded Transoxiana several times, it was only in 1089 under Sultan Malikshah, son of Alp Arslan, that they took Bukhara and then extended their sway throughout Transoxiana.

In retrospect, we can see that the fall of the Samanids did not bring about the greatest change in Khurasan, but it was rather the retreat of the Ghaznavids in favor of the nomadic Turks, the Seljüks, which opened a truly different page in history. After all, the Ghaznavids had begun as vassals of the Samanids and they maintained as much of the traditions and the organization of the Samanid kingdom as they could.

They even upheld Islamic orthodoxy when it was apparent that a majority of the population was not similarly inclined. The growth of Sufi orders and Shi'ite organizations in the eleventh century has been mentioned briefly, but the extent of such growth is hardly known, although it must have been greater than we learn from our sources.

We learn from Abu Sa'id, a famous Sufi or dervish of the early Seljük period in Nishapur, that the Sufis of Khurasan and Transoxiana were in close contact with each other, and that the Seljük leaders were under the influence of Sufis. This may account for a certain popular sentiment in favor of the Seljüks, as opposed to the Ghaznavids. The meeting place (*khanaqah*) of those Sufis who were followers of Abu Sa'id was the largest in Nishapur, but there were many others. The growth of the mystical orders in the Islamic world in the eleventh and twelfth centuries is well known. The great theologian al-Ghazzali, who died in 1111, was able to reconcile the Sufi movement with orthodox Islam, but the two nonetheless drew apart more and more in the following centuries. To follow the religious developments in Khurasan, including the resurgence of Isma'ilism, however, would lead us far from Bukhara. Yet it is important to note that the Isma'ili caliphate of the Fatimids had been established in Egypt and was active in sending missionaries to the eastern Islamic world. This missionary effort was especially important in Iran in the early eleventh century and it undoubtedly reached Bukhara and Transoxiana.

The trends of the time have been noted, and Bukhara did participate in the general history of the Islamic world. But in the time of the Seljüks, Transoxiana occupied a peripheral place in the affairs of the great sultans. The focus of attention shifted to the west, never to return, for in the general histories of the Islamic world, Central Asia is mentioned merely as the birthplace of the Moghul dynasty of India. Otherwise little is known about the land of Transoxiana which came to be called Turkistan. The Ottomans on the Mediterranean coasts and the Safavids in Persia became the two poles of the Islamic world and Transoxiana was forgotten. But everything is relative to the viewer, in our case looking from the west, far from Central Asia. And for the local inhabitants the cities of Samarqand and Bukhara continued to flourish, the former for a time with a special brilliance as the capital of Timur or Tamerlane and his successors. It may have seemed to some of the population that the golden age was long past, but the majority of contemporaries, as usual, could not discern the course of history, and would hardly pronounce their present or future a decline. From some points of view, of course, they were justified, but then history is many faceted, hence so intriguing. Again we have left the story of Bukhara, and must return in the next chapter to internal affairs of the city in the aftermath of the fall of the Samanids.

170

· 8 ·

The Iranian Legacy

> There were men in our day, not like the
> present breed. They were heroes, not you.
> LERMONTOV

INFORMATION about the cultural life of Bukhara and Transoxiana after the fall of the Samanids is unfortunately very
scant. The literature in Persian and Arabic from the period
of the Qarakhanids does not help us much, although the
continuation of past traditions is evident. Even among the
works of poetry we have little preserved, the *divan* or collection of the poet of Samarqand Suzani being the only
complete work in poetry from the Qarakhanid domain, although we have the names and fragments of many other
poets. It would seem that the high esteem held for poets
under the Samanids and Ghaznavids did not continue so
strongly under the Qarakhanids, which would parallel the
reputed piety of the khans and the increased authority of the
religious leaders in that period. The religious leaders never
regarded poets kindly.

There is, on the other hand, a good deal preserved in prose,
anthologies, and other compilatory works from the Qarakhanid period. For example, towards the close of this era,
Muhammad 'Aufi, author of an important collection of
biographies of poets, the *Lubab al-Albab,* and a collection of
stories, the *Jawami' al-Hikayat,* grew up in Bukhara *ca.*

1176–1200. The book on rhetoric, *Tarjuman al-Balagha,* by a certain Muhammad b. 'Umar Raduyani, may have been written at a Qarakhanid court about 1106, and Narshakhi's history of Bukhara was translated into Persian in 1128. May we call this an age of translation and compilation, similar to the Hellenistic period after the Classical Age of Greece?

This is not the place to discuss literary developments in any detail, but two tentative hypotheses relating to the Persian language and literature may be proposed here. First, the movement of poets and literary men which, in the early Samanid period, as we have seen, was to Khurasan and the east, with the capital city of Bukhara a strong magnet for talented people, seems to be reversed in the Qarakhanid period. Second, the Persian language, which was written in two styles, *Dari,* or pure Persian, and *Farsi,* or Arabic mixed with Persian, if we use general characteristics to define style, became more unified in a dominant *Farsi* style, with *Dari* losing its standing.

The migration of scholars and literary men from Transoxiana to the west, or even to India, is attested by the career of Ibn Sina in the early eleventh century, by the family of Nizami 'Arudi Samarqandi, author of the book *Chahar Maqale,* written in 1157, and by the poet Dhahir of Faryab, who began his career at the Qarakhanid court of Samarqand and then went to the west, ending his life at Tabriz. The influx of scholars and poets to India from Khurasan and Transoxiana, although ever increasing after the Mongol conquests, nonetheless began earlier. The grammarian al-Zamakhshari, born in Khwarazm but spending most of his life outside of Transoxiana only to return to his homeland to die in 1144, is not atypical. There were many others, but the trend away from Transoxiana is not extraordinary in view of the cultural and religious milieu in Transoxiana under the Qarakhanids.

The Arabicization of the Persian language is also not unexpected, for the linguistic situation in Khurasan and Transoxiana would favor such a development. We must remember that the literate classes in the eastern Islamic world were primarily the religious leaders and the scribes or bureaucrats, the former characterized as those who used Arabic in their writings, for the most part; the latter using Persian, either the *Dari* or *Farsi* style. One of the prime ministers of Mahmud of Ghazna in 1014 had ordered Arabic to replace Persian in all official correspondence, but the move was not popular and did not last long. Many scholars agree, however, that at the court of Ghazna the influence of Arabic was stronger than it had been at Bukhara. Perhaps the hypothesis proposed here best elucidates the subsequent development, namely the growth of *Farsi* at the expense of both *Dari* and Arabic. One may presume that by this date the reading public was accustomed to an Arabicized Persian, which had also become the written *lingua franca* of the eastern Islamic world.

Some writers might try to imitate Firdosi, but *Farsi* was the language of written communication, even though Turkish monarchs spoke their own dialects. Arabic remained the language of religion, even though *Farsi* flourished in the area of commentaries to the holy book and in philosophical and theological writings. Later *Farsi* was to become even more embellished with Arabic phrases, many of which were rare and archaic even to the eyes of literate Arabs. This amalgamation of Arabic and Persian remained until modern times. Attempts to eliminate Arabic from Persian have been as futile as any elimination of Latin and French influences in English.

The religious development in Transoxiana requires further study, but a preliminary sketch here may be of interest. In general one may describe the religious picture as a dual one. The orthodox Sunni religious leaders became stronger and, especially in Bukhara, more influential in political affairs. At the same time heretical movements were not unknown and the parallel growth of mystical orders seemed to belie the power and hold of the orthodox *'ulama* over the populace. Compared with the rest of Iran, however, Transoxiana remained a strong bastion of Sunni orthodoxy. The relations between the state and the religious leaders are of special interest and need some elaboration.

We have seen that certain families of religious leaders in Bukhara, such as the one of Abu Hafs in the beginning of Samanid rule, had acquired a high reputation and a great influence among the people. From time to time the activities of the religious leaders receive brief notices in the sources dealing with the Samanids, but we have very little information about them. On several occasions it seems as though the military and the religious leaders made a working agreement to accomplish a common purpose, and with the decline of the power of the rulers this alliance was apparently the real power behind the throne. Although the strength of the military class was obvious, the religious leaders did control the masses in some measure.

One detail revealing the growth of influence of the religious class was the increasing number of grand mosques, or Friday gathering mosques, even in small towns. Narshakhi mentions the villages where Friday mosques existed, including Iskijkath, where the grand mosque was built in the time of the Qarakhanid Nasr b. Ibrahim, called Shams al-Mulk (1068–80). Earlier the people of the town of Varakhsha had protested that they did not need a Friday mosque when *amir* Isma'il wanted them to build one. The same ruler, Shams al-Mulk, gave some of his royal estates to scholars of the Islamic religion, the revenues from which supported them. This and other such activities indicate a certain favor shown to some religious leaders in this period, even though on the whole the Qarakhanids opposed them.

When the Qarakhanids conquered Transoxiana, they were still close to their nomadic background and had to rely upon the Iranian bureaucracy, developed under the Samanids, to rule the cities and the settled countryside for them. 'Ali Tigin, for example, lived in an encampment near Bukhara called Kharlukh Ordu, according to his coins dated after 1026, and other Qarakhanids, too, kept away from the cities, considering the nomadic life more appropriate and better for them than the urban life of the Iranians. This meant that their lieutenants managed the urban centers. But when the nomadic army, encamped in the countryside, replaced the ruler and his guard in the city as the real authority, the way was open for another institution of authority and power to develop in the void left in the city. The religious leaders filled that void and thus they created a state within a state, but this happened later.

It would be useful to briefly summarize the change in the authority of the scribes or bureaucracy and of the religious leaders under Qarakhanid rule. The Qarakhanids originally had been converted to Islam by missionaries who were none too orthodox and by Sufis, so when they came to power they mistrusted the established, orthodox divines, the *'ulama*. As we have mentioned, they relied instead upon the bureaucracy or scribes *(dabir)* and thus were in constant strife with the religious leaders. After the Qarakhanids submitted to the overlordship of the Qara-Khitay rulers, the *'ulama* were exalted over the scribes. The change that occurred is well illustrated by two stories in the first discourse of the twelfth-century book, the *Four Discourses* of Samarqandi. In story eleven, he tells of a message sent from Mahmud of Ghazna to one of the Qarakhanid rulers, asking him to seek answers from the *'ulama* of his domain to such questions as the nature of Islam, of justice, right and wrong, and the like. The Qarakhanid, wishing to send answers which would provoke admiration at the court of Ghazna, asked his religious leaders to compose replies to the questions. Four months passed and a scribe, the secretary of the Qarakhanid ruler, finally composed an answer to all of the questions in a few words, "Reverence for God's command and loving-kindness towards God's people." This answer was much applauded at Ghazna, and the Qarakhanid ruler was pleased because the difficulty had been overcome by a scribe and not left to the divines.

The later situation is revealed by story nine. The Qara-Khitay ruler, called the Gür Khan, after his victory at Qatwan, appointed a civil governor named Alptigin, who was the nephew of Atsiz the Khwarazmshah over Bukhara. When the Qara-Khitay troops entered Bukhara, the *sadr,* or chief religious authority, was the son of 'Abd al-'Aziz b. 'Umar. He was killed during some opposition to the Qara-Khitay army, but was replaced by his brother Ahmad, who occupied the office of *sadr* until 1156. Alptigin oppressed the people of Bukhara so some of them went to the Gür Khan to protest. The latter wrote a succinct note to Alptigin say-ing, "let Alptigin do that which Ahmad commands, and Ahmad that which Muhammad [the prophet] commands." This indicates the shift in real authority from the bureauc-racy to the religious establishment in Bukhara.

We already have alluded to the influence and standing of certain families in different cities in Khurasan and Transoxi-ana. In Bukhara one family of judges attained leadership over the others during the Qarakhanid period, and eventu-ally the family came to rule the city. This was the famous Al-i Burhan, as it is called in the sources. Before they came to power, however, another family paved the way for the institution of chief religious leader of Bukhara to become firmly established. This predecessor was the family of the Isma'ili *imams.*

A Persian book called the history of Mullazade, written in the early fifteenth century, tells of the graves and mauso-leums of the learned and pious men of Bukhara. Among them was a family of *imams* or religious leaders called Isma'ili. To quote the book:

"In the northern part of the road of the gate of the pil-grims, opposite the shrine of Abu Bakr Fadl, was the tomb of the Isma'ili *imams.* The author of the book *Ansab* says they were known and famous in Bukhara, and their tomb was by the Khurasan road." Further, Abu Bakr Ahmad b. Muhammad b. Isma'il was born in 913 and died in 994. His son was Abu'l-Hasan 'Ali b. Ahmad, and his grandson, Abu Bakr Sa'd, who died in 1010. Hafiz Ghunjar mentioned him in his history, and regarding Abu'l-Hasan he said, "His father was the [leading] elder and mayor of the time, and the religious leader of his age in Transoxiana. The office of mayor and of *imam* was transmitted from him to Abu'l-Hasan his son after 1000, for he had the skill and merit for this position."

This family, in its period of ascendancy, was the ruling power in Bukhara, similar to the Mikalis in Nishapur, and similar families in other cities. I have used the word "mayor" for *ra'is* or "chief," although the contemporary office in American cities is only a very rough translation. Not unexpectedly these religious leaders, who were political leaders as well, clashed with their Qarakhanid overlords. We do not know whether the Qarakhanid government had the right to remove the *imam* and *ra'is* of Bukhara, but we hear of another family, the Saffari *imams*, holding this rank later, indicating a change. In 1069 Abu Ibrahim Isma'il al-Saffar, who held the joint office of *imam* and *ra'is*, was executed by Shams al-Mulk. His son Abu Ishaq b. Isma'il, who presumably succeeded his father, was just as critical of the Qarakhanids and a thorn in their flesh, as was his father. Abu Ishaq seems to have occupied his high post until Sultan Sanjar, the Seljük ruler, intervened in Transoxiana. The Seljük sultan, in order to curb the critical *imam* and restore peace, took Abu Ishaq to Merv about 1102. At the same time or shortly thereafter, Sanjar appointed his own brother-in-law, 'Abd al-'Aziz b. 'Umar al-Maza, a learned religious leader of Merv, as head of the judges and religious establishment in Bukhara to replace Abu Ishaq. 'Abd al-'Aziz was given the title of *sadr* and the *laqab* of Burhan al-Millah wa'l-Din, as well as others. This was the beginning of the family dynasty of religious leaders in Bukhara called Al-i Burhan after his *laqab*. So the Al-i Burhan succeeded previous families in the leadership of affairs in Bukhara.

In 1102 Sanjar defeated and killed a prince of the eastern line of the Qarakhanids, Qadir Khan, who had proclaimed himself supreme ruler of the west Qarakhanid state in Transoxiana. Sanjar then installed another Qarakhanid prince called Arslan Khan as his vassal over Transoxiana. This Arslan Khan, who ruled until 1130, was a great builder, and under him the large minaret of Bukhara was restored, lasting down to the present day. He also restored the grand mosque and the garden or place of festival prayers, which had formerly been the site of the villas and gardens of Shamsabad where Shams al-Mulk resided. Arslan Khan also constructed baths and palaces and rebuilt the walls of the city. He rebuilt much of the town of Paikand at the southernmost part of the oasis of Bukhara, but his failure to provide an adequate water supply made his efforts short-lived. A quarrel broke out between Arslan Khan and Sanjar, with the result that Sanjar besieged Samarqand, where Arslan Khan was staying. Arslan Khan was succeeded by another member of the Qarakhanid dynasty, who ruled a short time and then was replaced by another prince called

Qilich Tamgach Khan, also an appointee of Sanjar. The
Seljüks had become the rulers of Transoxiana, and the Qarakhanid princes were merely vassals of Sanjar.

Sanjar, however, had other troubles; among them he had
to fight a rebellious vassal, Atsiz, the ruler of Khwarazm.
Although the Sultan was successful, the danger from Atsiz
was not removed, and the Khwarazmshah in 1139 was able
to capture Bukhara, kill Sanjar's governor, and destroy the
citadel. Soon afterwards he came to terms and made peace
with Sanjar and submitted to him. Shortly afterwards Sanjar
marched to meet an invasion of the infidel Qara-Khitay people from the Far East, but in September, 1141, the Seljüks
were completely routed at a battle in the Qatwan steppe near
Samarqand. The entire country fell into the hands of the
pagan Qara-Khitay rulers, who occupied Bukhara the same
year.

The Qara-Khitay ruler did not change the *status quo* in
Transoxiana, since one of the Qarakhanid princes, Ibrahim
b. Muhammad, became the *kagan* as a vassal of the Qara-
Khitay. Ibrahim, however, was killed in a battle with some
Qarluq Turks near Bukhara in 1156. Qarakhanid princes
under Qara-Khitay rule continued to exercise authority, but
they were greatly weakened in power. In Bukhara the *sadrs*
managed affairs of the city, although Qarakhanid princes
were nominally the civil governors.

Early in the period of Qara-Khitay rule, the Oghuz Turks,
from whom the Seljüks arose, captured Bukhara and destroyed the citadel, though they remained in possession of
the city only a short time. The citadel had been destroyed
earlier by the Khwarazmshah and then rebuilt by Alptigin

early in the rule of the Qara-Khitay. The activities of the Qarluqs and Oghuz, as well as other Turkish tribes, indicate the unsettled condition of life in Transoxiana and Khurasan. The Oghuz plundered Merv, Nishapur, and other cities of Khurasan, including Balkh in 1155, where they wreaked much havoc. At this time in the west, the Crusaders became familiar with the "feudal system" of Muslim princes, similar to conditions in western Europe, and they also learned of a pagan ruler who had conquered Muslims in the east. This was an echo of the Qara-Khitay defeat of Sanjar.

To summarize the events relating to Bukhara in the last half of the twelfth century, one may describe the period as a series of struggles between the Qarluqs, the Khwarazmshahs, and the Qara-Khitays allied with Qarakhanid princes. The Al-i Burhan family really continued to rule Bukhara in spite of the change of civil governors. Muhammad b. 'Umar, son of the *imam* who was killed in 1141, is called mayor *(ra'is)* of Bukhara in the sources, and he co-operated with the Qarakhanids in the decisive defeat of the Qarluqs about 1158. The earlier conflicts between the Qarakhanids and the religious leaders seem to have been resolved in later years, possibly in some measure because of the need for the union of all the Muslims who were under pagan Qara-Khitay rule. One of the Qarakhanid rulers, Mas'ud b. 'Ali, repaired the walls of Bukhara in this period but not the citadel.

In 1182 the troops of the Khwarazmshah Takash captured Bukhara after a short siege, and the religious leaders, as well as most of the population, were not loath to transfer their loyalties from infidel overlords to Muslims. Khwarazmian rule, however, did not last long and Qarakhanid rule, under Qara-Khitay overlordship, was soon restored. It should be mentioned that the seat of rule of the Qarakhanid princes was in Samarqand, and Bukhara was theoretically under the jurisdiction of Samarqand. The power of the *sadrs* of the Al-i Burhan, however, continually increased until they were almost independent. They collected tribute for the Qara-Khitay rulers, but we do not know whether they at first sent the tribute through the Qarakhanid ruler in Samarqand, although later it would seem they sent it directly to the Gür Khan.

The *sadrs* of the Al-i Burhan, who held both the religious and civil authority of Bukhara in their hands, became very wealthy. One author, Muhammad al-Nasawi, in his biography of the last Khwarazmshah, tells of the wealth of the *sadr* Burhan al-Din Muhammad b. Ahmad b. 'Abd al-'Aziz about 1205:

"When one heard that he was the chief preacher of Bukhara, one could understand that he was like other chief preachers in his exalted rank, and that he would own large domains and great estates. . . . But the situation was not like that; rather one could only compare him with the greatest of lords and the strongest of kings, for he had more than six thousand *faqihs* [students of law and judges] under his orders and in his charge." His wealth and his pride did not endear him to those he met in Baghdad when he made the pilgrimage to Mecca in 1207, although he was said to be a generous man. The relations of the *sadrs* with the Qarakhanid rulers in ruling Bukhara are not discussed in the sources, but we may assume that authority was in the hands of the former, while the latter ruled in name.

Coins minted in Bukhara with the name of the west Qarakhanid ruler, Ibrahim b. Husain, dating from 1201, exist, indicating at least a nominal Qara-Khitay overlordship there. Shortly afterwards the son of Ibrahim, 'Uthman Khan, became ruler in Samarqand but apparently Bukhara was not under him since we do not find coins of his struck in Bukhara. We learn instead of a man of the common folk called Sanjar, the son of a shield seller, who seized control of the civil authority. Several sources say he held the upper classes in contempt, and probably the Al-i Burhan were among them. They complained to the Qara-Khitay ruler about Sanjar, who had taken the title of king, but the Gür Khan was not able to intervene. So they turned to the Khwarazmshah.

The Khwarazmshah, who was Muhammad b. Takash, took Bukhara about 1209 and put an end to Malik Sanjar, as he was called. The former, however, did not restore the authority to the *sadr* Muhammad b. Ahmad b. 'Abd al-'Aziz, but rather sent him as a prisoner to Khwarazm. The Khwarazmshah then appointed an outsider, Majd al-Din al-Farawi, to be chief of the Hanafite judges of Bukhara, while a lieutenant of the Khwarazmshah was given the civil and military authority as governor. The Khwarazmians continued on the road to Samarqand, which they took, and later they defeated the Qara-Khitays. The rule of the Muslim Khwarazmians, however, was no better than that of the infidel Qara-Khitays, to judge from accounts of their relations with the inhabitants of Samarqand. In 1212 the latter massacred all of the Khwarazmians they could find, but the Khwarazmshah soon appeared with his army and after a short siege captured and sacked the city. The ruling Qara-khanid prince, 'Uthman, and members of his family were executed. This was the end of the Qarakhanid dynasty in Transoxiana, while the Qara-Khitays had replaced them elsewhere.

Khwarazmian rule was not to last long in Bukhara or anywhere, for a conflict with the Mongol successors of the Qara-Khitay, as well as other rulers, brought an end to the Khwarazmian dynasty and marked the end of Muslim rule in all of Central Asia and Iran. In March, 1220, the Mongol army of Chinggis *kagan* appeared before the gates of Bukhara. After a long siege of the citadel, in which the people of Bukhara were driven by the Mongols against the defenders of the citadel, the Mongol army was victorious. Most of the city was burned and the slaughter of the populace was enormous, although not as complete as elsewhere. The Mongol conquest of Bukhara marked the end of an epoch. Bukhara soon recovered, but the destruction wrought by the Mongols in all the land left a permanent scar across the face of Central Asia and Iran. The shock of an infidel conquest of most of the lands of the eastern Islamic world was to remain with the Muslims for generations. For Bukhara the medieval achievement was over in 1220.

To recapitulate: the period between 1000 and 1220 saw Bukhara and all of Transoxiana change from being the frontier of Islam and Iran against the Turks, to an important part of the Central Asian Islamic world. After 1220

Transoxiana became the southern part of the Central Asian Turko-Mongol world. Bukhara before 1000 was connected with Baghdad; after 1220 it was connected with Kashgar, then with Qaraqorum in Mongolia, and with China. The entire direction of Bukhara and Transoxiana had shifted from south to north. Likewise, the ethnic and cultural relations of Bukhara changed, since the city came within the boundaries of a new Turkistan. The Turkish language did not replace Persian, but the two existed side by side and many, perhaps a majority of the people, were bi-lingual, just as earlier many knew both Arabic and Persian. Just as the literature of the Samanid period had been one literature in two languages, so after the Mongol conquest we find poets able to compose in both Turkish and Persian. The Turks had become an important part of the Islamic world, which took shape as a tripartite aspect of Turks, Persians, and Arabs. This division lasted down to our day.

The Turkish literary output was far surpassed by Persian and Arabic, of course, but the Qarakhanid period in the history of Central Asia is noteworthy for the creation of an Islamic Turkish literature. Few of the literary productions have survived, but those which have are impressive in their scope and style. Perhaps the most famous of the literary productions of the Qarakhanid period was the "Mirror for Princes," called the *Qutadgu Bilig,* or "Knowledge for Attaining the Charisma [of kingship]." It was written in Kashgar by a certain Yusuf from Balasagun for a Qarakhanid ruler, Tamgach Bughra Khan, in 1069. This Turkish book compares favorably with the Persian *Siyasat Name* of Nizam al-Mulk and other works of this genre, but there is a fundamental difference between the two. The Qarakhanids were members of an old Turkic ruling dynasty maintaining old Turkic traditions. These traditions were preserved even after the Islamification of the Qarakhanids. The Turkic literary language which arose and flourished under the Qarakhanids was an Islamic literary language after the model of New Persian, and the basic influence on this Turkic literature was the New Persian Islamic literature developed under the Samanids. So the *Qutadgu Bilig* joined the Persian Islamic tradition with the Central Asian Turkic tradition. This is why Qarakhanid literature was so important. It was the background for all later Islamic Turkic literatures in Central Asia and even in Anatolia.

The Seljüks, on the other hand, were *condottieri* who did not hold to old Turkic dynastic traditions. They quite rapidly became Iranicized and the *Siyasat Name* could have been written for Iranian rulers such as the Boyids as well as for Turkish rulers. The Seljüks were not the same as the Qarakhanids and certainly in no way as important for the future development of Turkish literature or culture.

Another work of great importance is the dictionary of words of Turkish dialects explained in Arabic by Mahmud al-Kashgari, written in Baghdad about 1073. Turkish, just like Persian in an earlier period, as a language greatly increased in richness and scope when it became an Islamic tongue. Bukhara did not really participate in the development of Turkish as a vehicle of Islamic literature and thought, for the city in the Zarafshan basin was too much bound to the Iranian traditions of the past, and it continued to be a center of Persian. The flowering of Turkish occurred

to the east of Transoxiana in Kashgar, Balasagun, and elsewhere, and is not properly a part of our story.

The building activity of the Qarakhanids, however, is
an interesting feature of that era which deserves mention.
The interest in building large mosques, schools, caravansarais, and mausoleums was characteristic not only of the
Qarakhanid rulers, but also of the Seljüks and Ottoman
Turks. Perhaps the Islamic Turkish rulers wanted to show
their devotion to their religion, or sought to preserve their
names in their buildings, so we have many magnificent
structures in the Islamic world built by Turkish princes.
Among the interesting buildings in the city of Bukhara and
its oasis from the Qarakhanid period are a caravansarai in
the oasis called Rabat-i Malik, built by Shams al-Mulk about
1075. The famous grand minaret of the chief mosque of
Bukhara, rebuilt under Arslan Khan in 1127, has been mentioned and is one of the tourist sights of Bukhara. The intricate geometric designs in brickwork on the minaret give
a good example of the style of the age when it was built. The
geometric designs on the alabaster facing around the central place of festival prayers (*namazgah*) in Bukhara and
similar facing on the mosque of Magoki Attar both date
from the early twelfth century, and are also fine examples of
the elaborate style of decoration characteristic of the art of
the Qarakhanid period. Another feature of Qarakhanid
architecture is the widespread use of terra cotta slabs, also
with intricately interwoven geometric designs, on buildings
of all kinds. Traces of wall paintings found in a villa dating
from this era in Termez indicate the continuance of the
tradition of painting, even of human forms contrary to Islam,

from pre-Islamic times down to the Mongol conquest. The use of colored glass, new architectural features, and developments in bronze and copper work attest the artistic importance of the lands under Qarakhanid rule in the history of Islamic culture. Again only the most general remarks can be made here, for the subject of Islamic art is vast and needs much more study than hitherto given it.

To turn to the religious developments in Bukhara under the Qarakhanids, the strong adherence to Sunni orthodoxy of the Hanafite school of law, the dominating force, is mentioned by the sources. Bukhara, as we have seen, was the center of the Hanafites in Transoxiana, although they also were strong elsewhere. The decentralization of authority under the Qarakhanids, however, enabled Shi'ites to spread their doctrines, and Sufism also was popular. In fact the growth of *waqfs* or endowments for mosques, *medresas,* dervish halls and other religious establishments made the religious leaders custodians of increasing amounts of land and wealth. The yearly income of the *sadr* 'Umar b. 'Abd al-'Aziz was enormous, and was derived not only from land but also ownership of shops in the bazaars, baths, caravansarais, and other establishments. Certainly the position of the religious leaders in Transoxiana and in Bukhara, more than elsewhere, grew in importance far beyond what it previously had been. This position was to be maintained in the years after the Mongol conquest, even though never equal to the peak of *sadr* rule in Bukhara in the eleventh century.

The development of higher religious schools or colleges has been mentioned when speaking of the Samanids, but it was only under the Qarakhanids that Bukhara became

famous as the center of orthodox Sunni Hanafite learning,
and to its schools came students from all over Central Asia
and Iran. From its schools went men learned in religious
law, logic, philosophy, and other branches of learning. We
have no direct evidence, but it would seem that Bukhara
had one of the oldest, if not the very oldest of schools of
higher learning in the Islamic world. When Nizam al-Mulk
established the famous Nizamiyya College in Baghdad, he
most probably was copying an eastern Iranian institution.
The origin is sometimes attributed to Balkh, but Bukhara in
my opinion would be a better candidate as the home of the
medresa. Unfortunately our sources fail us on this point.

It is difficult to determine whether the common folk had
better living conditions under the Samanids than under
the Qarakhanids. The silver crisis continued down to the
Mongol conquest, and if foreign trade is a good index of
prosperity in this period, there certainly was a drop in ex-
changes with eastern Europe. The almost total absence of
post-Samanid coins in the Russian and Scandinavian coin
hoards points to a cessation of trade. This would parallel
the fall of the Khazar Kingdom in the north Caucasus area
and the invasion of Turkish tribes known as Qipchaks and
Polovtsi into the steppes of South Russia. The proliferation
of robber bands, *'ayyar*, plus the Turkish nomadic tribes
throughout the Near East are characteristic of this age, which
many scholars have characterized as one of decline. Curi-
ously, as we have seen with the artistic flowering under the
Qarakhanids, so elsewhere in Iran the time between the fall
of the Samanids and the Mongol invasion was a period of
great literary, especially poetic, activity. In the eastern part of

Iran alone one might mention Sana'i, Mu'izzi, 'Umar Khay-yam, and Anwari as a few of the poets who were active in this period.

From our point of view perhaps the most significant feature of the history of the Qarakhanids was the beginning of the settlement of Turkish tribes on the land in Transoxiana. The process of mixture and assimilation between the Turkish and Iranian speakers, of course, lasted many centuries, but soon the Sogdians, Khwarazmians, and others became Turkish (and Persian) speakers. As we learn from Mahmud al-Kashgari and other sources, there were many Turkish dialects spoken in Central Asia in the eleventh century. The various Iranian dialects, even in the countryside, were giving ground to Persian, so the future situation was already in formation in the Qarakhanid period. When the Özbeks invaded Transoxiana from the north at the end of the fifteenth century, they were merely to give their name to a Turkistan already in existence. I also would like to emphasize the important role played by the Turks in the change from the *Dari* style of Persian to the *Farsi* style in Central Asia. The mixture of Arabic and Persian seems to have accelerated during Qarakhanid rule, which can be attributed to the expanding influence of the religious leaders as well as the *medresas*. Furthermore, the Turkish rulers might have favored a greater Arabic-Persian mixture in the Persian tongue of their subjects for political as well as religious reasons.

It remains to assess the Iranian legacy in Bukhara and in Transoxiana. When we remember that the Iranian area before Islam was essentially divided into two main parts, a west-

ern with its center in Fars province and an eastern with its
center, at least some of the time, in Balkh, we can better keep
in perspective the position of Bukhara throughout history.
Until the Arab conquests, Bukhara's southern axis was
towards Balkh and over the Hindu Kush mountains to India.
The empires of the Kushans and the Hephtalites gave the
political framework for the cultural and ethnic affinities of
the axis. If we consider the large east Iranian cultural area
as a unity in regard to its geographical position, and in trade
and commerce, we may say that the four principal oases were
oriented differently. Balkh looked to trade with India;
Samarqand sent merchants to China; Khwarazm maintained
contacts with the North Caucasus and the Volga; while
Bukhara was closely connected to Merv and the Sasanian
Empire to the west. Probably Bukhara was more under west
Iranian influences than the other three, and consequently
the city had a special role to play in the amalgamation of
western and eastern Iran under Muslim rule. For the Arabs
were not merely the heirs of the Sasanians; they extended
their frontiers much further than had their predecessors. In
effect they brought all of the Iranian cultural area under the
one roof of the caliphate. Bukhara became a center, if not
the center, for the fusion of east and west. It was also the
Arab stronghold in Transoxiana where a large Arab garrison was permanently settled. This settlement must have provided the nucleus or basis on which Bukhara built its reputation as the dome of Islam in the east, a veritable second
Baghdad. Bukhara was the meeting point of three cultures,
not just two as elsewhere, the west Iranian, the Arab-Muslim,
and the east Iranian. This, in my opinion, is the main reason

why it became the great center it did in the tenth century. It must be stressed that the careful delineation of three cultures must be understood in general terms, for there was much overlapping, and geographical boundaries were mostly artificial or arbitrary, viewed in the light of such a division. Nonetheless I feel that the happy concordance of three cultural strands in medieval Bukhara provided the background for the rise of that civilization which can be called the New Persian Renaissance when concentrating on language and literature, or the eastern Islamic culture when concerned with art and thought. Both organized Sufi mysticism and the institution of higher education (*medresa*) came from eastern Iran. So did Ibn Sina, al-Biruni, Firdosi, and many others. Transoxiana and Bukhara contributed mightily to the world civilization we call Islamic, and they were the places where the Turks were first educated when they came into the Islamic world.

The first Islamic Turkish empire, of the Qarakhanids, ruled Transoxiana, and it was different from the Ghaznavid state, which was basically Iranian with Turkish rulers. By 1000 A.D., when I use the term Iranian, I mean that new combination which was developed in Transoxiana from the old east and west Iranian traditions plus Arab Islam. This was the rich fare of which the Turks partook when they became converted to Islam, and the Turks themselves contributed a new element to the melting pot. The new amalgam was accomplished primarily in Central Asia where later a separation from the Iranian world took place. For the wheel of history seemed to have turned after the Mongol conquests, and, after a short period of unity, Central Asia and Transoxiana again broke away from the west and two areas formed, similar to the situation in pre-Islamic times. Only now it was not east and west Iranian, but a Central Asian or Turkish culture fused with pan-Iranian culture as opposed to a pan-Iranian area on the plateau. And the two drifted further apart in the course of time. Under the Safavids, Shi'ism became the state religion on the Iranian plateau and a kind of rejection of the Turkish element in the melting pot occurred. In Transoxiana, however, with the expansion of the Özbeks, the opposite process developed —a strengthening of Turkish elements and Sunni orthodoxy. So in a sense the ancient pre-Islamic difference between east and west reappeared and continued down to the present.

Under the Özbek rulers, Bukhara experienced a revival, but it was local, without influence on Iran or the Arab world. The old unity had been broken. Some of the finest architectural remains in Bukhara date from the period of Özbek rule, and the sixteenth to eighteenth centuries saw an economic and cultural growth in the city. Before this period, under Timur and his successors, Bukhara was flourishing, although not as much as Timur's capital, Samarqand. Interesting events took place under Timur; for example, the famous Naqshbandi order of dervishes was founded in Bukhara by Baha al-Din Naqshbandi, who died in 1388. But to recount the history of Bukhara from the Mongol invasion to the present would be another, and more voluminous, story. The pre-Mongol period has been merely skimmed, and even in it much of interest has been omitted. The story of the Jews of Bukhara and the Marranos, or Judeo-Muslims, would require a monograph. The Jews were probably settled in

Bukhara for a long time, although their origins are unknown. They seem to have been a significant part of the population down to the present. Like the Jews in Iran, they participated in and contributed to the prevailing civilization, using Persian as their language of communication. The existence of various strata of Islamicized Jews is a fascinating example of mixture, and of the adaptability of the Jewish people.

Likewise the Arabs of Bukhara, who have been the subject of many recent studies by Soviet scholars, present many problems in their long history of a separate existence in villages of the oasis and elsewhere in Transoxiana. Some Arabs are probably descendants of late migrants to the area, while others are descendants of earlier ones, but much remains to be done in elucidating their history. The gypsies in the oasis of Bukhara too require further study.

Many questions might be raised about the later history of Bukhara after the Mongol invasion which we cannot discuss here. The lovely muted red Bukhara rugs of recent times, for example, probably were the result of Özbek taste and nomadic Türkmen weaving techniques, although we have little direct evidence of their origins. The survival of cultural institutions in Bukhara after the thirteenth century, in spite of later invasions and turmoil, in my opinion, is the result of the happy marriage of Islamic-Persian and Turkic traditions under the Qarakhanids. Just as under the Samanids there was formed one Islamic culture using two languages, Arabic and Persian, so under the Qarakhanids that Islamic culture was blended with Turkic traditions to form another Islamic culture using two languages, Persian and Turkish.

This latter amalgam was the lasting monument of the Qarakhanids upon which the Özbeks built. Thus cultural continuity was assured.

To deal in detail with the above questions would require another book, and rather than continue with such tantalizing tidbits, it would be better to end our story of medieval Bukhara with two typical Muslim conclusions to books: "What has been told is in part, not all," and "God alone knows best."

Selecteδ Bibliography

CONTEMPORARY SOURCES:

1. The basic work is Narshakhi's *History of Bukhara,* of which we have preserved only an abridgement made by a certain Muhammad b. Zufar b. 'Umar in 1178 of a Persian translation made by Abu Nasr Ahmad al-Qubavi in 1128 of the Arabic original made in 943. There are several editions of the work, a Russian translation, and an English translation by R. N. Frye in the Mediaeval Academy of America series (Cambridge, Mass., 1954).

2. The second book relating to Bukhara is the *Kitab-i Mullazade,* or *Mazarat-i Bukhara,* "The Tombs of Bukhara," by a certain Mu'in al-Fuqara, written in Persian shortly after 1411. There are several editions of the work, including one by Ahmad Gulchin Ma'ani in Tehran, 1961. See also my article on the book in the *Avicenna Commemoration Volume* (Calcutta, 1956), 89–93.

3. For the early Islamic history of Bukhara, the great Arabic chronicle of Tabari is indispensable, with the Persian translation of the work by Bal'ami adding some new information. The former was edited in Leiden in thirteen volumes from 1879–1901 by M. de Goeje. The latter was translated into French by M. H. Zotenberg in four volumes (Paris, 1867–1874).

4. For the Samanids, we have the section on that dynasty from Mirkhond's world history in Persian, translated into

French by M. Defremery (Paris, 1845), and the *Ta'rikh-i Gozide* of Hamdallah Qazvini, also translated into French by J. Gantin (Paris, 1903). The history of Gardizi, in several editions, has not been translated.

5. For biographies of important inhabitants of Bukhara, see the *Kitab al-Ansab* of Sam'ani, edited in facsimile in the Gibb Memorial Series No. 20 (London, 1912). A new printed edition is in press in Hyderabad.

6. The most valuable of the Arabic geographical sources for Bukhara is the book by al-Maqdisi, edited by M. de Goeje in the series *Bibliotheca Geographorum Arabicorum* (Leiden, 1877). Other geographers in the same series have items of interest, while the geographical dictionary of Yaqut, edited by F. Wüstenfeld in six volumes (Leipzig, 1866–1873) is a mine of information on the villages of the oasis of Bukhara.

7. For the Qarakhanid period of the history of Transoxiana, the histories of Ibn al-Athir, ed. C. J. Tornberg (Leiden, 1867–1871), and of Juvaini, translated into English by J. A. Boyle under the title *History of the World Conqueror* (Harvard University Press, 1958) are of great importance.

8. The *Chahar Maqale,* or "Four Discourses," of Nizami-i 'Arudi Samarqandi has been translated into English by E. G. Browne, in the *Journal of the Royal Asiatic Society* for 1899.

A list of other sources may be found in the bibliography to my translation of Narshakhi's history.

MODERN STUDIES:

1. The basic work on Islamic Transoxiana is W. Barthold, *Turkestan Down to the Mongol Invasion* (London, 1928, new ed., 1958). Unfortunately, we have no study of the Samanids, and Barthold's work remains the standard study on them.

2. On the Ghaznavids, the book of C. E. Bosworth, *The Ghaznavids* (Edinburgh, 1963) is an excellent guide.

3. For the literary scene, including the rise of New Persian, the monumental work of E. G. Browne, *A Literary History of Persia,* in four volumes (Cambridge University Press, several editions), is still useful. More useful are the relevant pages in J. Rypka, *Iranische Literaturgeschichte* (Leipzig, 1959), 139–69. A specialized study of great importance is the work of E. Bertels, *Persidskaya Poeziya v Bukhare X vek,* Trudy Instituta Vostokovedeniya 10 (Moscow, 1935), 57 Pp.

4. The history of the Qarakhanids has been clarified by Omeljan Pritsak in a series of articles:

O. Pritsak, "The Decline of the Empire of the Oghuz Yabghu," *Annals of the Ukranian Academy of Arts and Sciences,* 2 (New York), 1952, 279–92.

———, "Karachanidische Streitfragen," *Oriens* 3 (1950), 209–28.

———, "Von den Karluk zu den Karachaniden," *ZDMG,* 101 (1951), 270–300.

———, "Āl-i Burhān," *Der Islam,* 30 (1952), 81–96.

5. Finally the new *Encyclopaedia of Islam* provides convenient references to many details in the present book.

Additional Bibliography to Second Edition

I now believe that the name "Bukhara" is related to the Sogdian word *fwq'r*, found in Christian texts and with the meaning
"glorious, distinguished." For further discussion see my article
on Bukhara in the *Encyclopaedia Iranica*, or in Paksoy, H.B.,
ed., *Central Asian Monuments* (Isis Press, Istanbul, 1992), 65-
71.

For general remarks and bibliography see my book *The
Heritage of Central Asia, From Antiquity to the Turkish Expansion* (Markus Wiener, Princeton, 1996). More specialized
works are the following:

Lazard, G., "Dari," in *Encyclopaedia Iranica*, Vol. VII, Mazda
    Publishers, 1996, 34-5.
Livshits, V.A., with Kaufman & Dyakonov, " O drevnei sogdi-
    iskoi pismennosti Bukhary," *Vestnik Drevnei Istorii*,
    1965, no. 3.
Negmatov, N. N., *Gosudarstvo Samanidov* (Moscow, 1977),
    with Tajik translation *Davlati Somonien* (Dushanbe,
    1989).
Smirnova, Olga I., *Svodnyi Katalog Sogdiiskikh Monet,
    bronza* (Moscow, 1981). esp. 426-8.
Rtveladze, E. V., *Drevnie Monety Srednei Azii* (Tashkent,
    1987), with English summary. Also his ed. of *Numismatik
    Tsentralnoi Azii* (Tashkent, 1995), esp., the article of A.I.
    Naimark on the beginning of copper coinage in Bukhara.
Zeimal, E.V., *Drevnie monety Tadzhikistana* (Dushanbe,
    1983).

Index

201

Index

Biruni, al-: 102, 104, 105–109, 192
Bishr b. Tughshada: 20
Böri Tigin: *see* Ibrahim b. Nasr
Bosworth: 122
Boyid: 86–87, 89–101, 124, 126, 139–42, 144, 146, 148, 168
Buddhism: 6, 99
Buddhist: 6, 27, 115
Bughra Khan: 143–45, 164
Bukhar Khudah: 12, 15–16, 22, 24–25, 27, 32, 48, 72, 153–54
Bukhari, Abu Bakr Akhavani: 103
Bulghars: 57, 71–72, 116, 132
Bumijkath: 3, 8
Bunyat b. Tughshada: 22–23, 25
Burhan, Al-i: 47, 131, 177, 179, 181–83
Burhan al-Din Muhammad b. Ahmad b. 'Abd al-'Aziz: 182
Bust: 128
Busurman: 71
Byzantine: 123–24, 140, 155, 168

Caspian: 41, 52, 86, 101, 139, 141
Caucasus: 118, 189, 191
Chaghani, Abu 'Ali: 86–87
Chaghani, Abu Mansur: 54
Chaghaniyan: 87, 95, 129, 146
Chagri Tigin: *see* Ja'far Tigin
Chahar Maqale: 172, 176
Ch'ang-ch'ien: 6
China: 6–7, 18, 21–22, 26, 29, 40, 70–73, 81, 83, 185, 191
Chinese Turkistan: 116; *see also* Sinkiang
Chinggis ḳagan: 184
Chosroes Anushirvan: 44, 102

Christian: 19, 115
Constantinople: 111
Crusade: 168, 181
Ctesiphon: 44
Cyrus: 4

Dabir: 74, 176
Damascus: 18, 21
Damghan: 86
Dandanqan: 166
Daqiqi, Abu Mansur Muhammad b. Ahmad: 95–96
Dari: 62, 63, 172, 173, 190; *see also* Persian, *Farsi*
Darius: 5
Daulatshah: 65
Davidovich, E. A.: 25
Daylam: 139
Demetrius: 5
Dhahir of Faryab: 172
Dihqan: 32, 35, 43, 48, 73–74, 90–92, 96, 100, 119, 123, 125, 151, 156–57
Dirhem: 25, 36, 154–55
Divan: 44, 46
Divan Lughat al-Tur ḳ: 112
Dizoi: 13

Egypt: 33, 119, 169
Emba River: 113
Euthydemus: 5

Faiq: 141–46
Fakhr al-Daulah: 142, 144–45
Faqih: 75, 86, 182
Farabi, al-: 58, 82
Faramurz, Shams al-Mulk: 101
Farazdak: 62

Fars: 98, 139–40, 191
Farsi: 62, 172–73, 190; *see also*
Persian, *Dari*
Fatimid: 52–53, 55, 140, 169
Ferghana: 35–36, 38, 40, 51, 70,
115
Fihrist: 115
Firdosi: 11, 27–28, 95–96, 97–101,
103, 173, 192
Firuzan: 101
Fityan: 125
Frunze: 40
Futuwa: 160

Galen: 108
Gandhara: 6
Garchistan: 146
Gardizi: 56, 88, 143
Garshasp Name: 100
German coins: 155
Ghazal: 64
Ghazis: 94, 115, 117, 123–24, 131,
149, 160
Ghazna: 88, 105–106, 128–29,
144–46, 173, 176
Ghaznavid: 44, 83, 85, 88, 96,
122, 124, 128, 133, 149, 162–63,
166–69, 171, 192
Ghazzali, al-: 169
Ghitrifi (coin): 25
Ghulam: 119, 128
Ghunjar, Hafiz: 178
Gilan: 139
Gird Name: 101
Greco-Bactrian: 5
Greek: 6, 68, 120–21, 172
Gujarat: 72
Gurgan: 141–42

Gurganj: 105, 145
Gür Khan: 176–77, 182–83

Hafiz: 64
Hafs, Khwaja Imam Abu: 47,
130, 174
Hajjaj b. Yusuf: 15
Hamadan: 86, 101, 107, 139, 162
Hamdallah Qazvini: 50
Hanafite: 47, 77, 80, 130–31,
134, 188–89
Harun al-Hasan b. Sulaiman: *see*
Bughra Khan
Hellenism: 29
Hephtalite: 8, 10–12, 191
Herat: 35, 65, 74, 129, 138, 142,
144, 146
Hermitage Museum: 13
Herodotus: 5, 111
Hidayat al-muta'allimin: 103
Hilal al-Sabi: 147
Hindu: 129
Hindu Kush: 154, 191
Hormizd IV: 13
Hsüan-tsang: 9
Husain b. Mansur, al-
(Qarakhanid): 164
Husain b. Tahir: 37–39

Ibn al-Athir: 124, 143, 162
Ibn al-Muqaffa': 62
Ibn al-Nadim: 115
Ibn al-Rumi: 62
Ibn Fadlan: 57, 71, 116
Ibn Hauqal: 121
Ibn Karram: 78, 130
Ibn Miskawaih: 124

Index

Bibliotheca Iranica, Reprint Series, consists of the following titles:

Qajar Iran
Political, Social, and Cultural Change 1800-1925
Edited by C.E. Bosworth and Carole Hillenbarnd
1992: xxv+414pp.,illus.,maps,index. [Unnumbered]
ISBN:0-939214-98-9(paper).

The Heritage of Persia
Richard N. Frye
1993: xiv+330pp.,illus.,bibl.,index. [No.1]
ISBN:1-56859-008-3(paper).

The Diary of H. M. The Shah of Persia
During His Tour Through Europe in A.D. 1873
J.W. Redhouse
New Introduction by
Carole Hillenbrand
1995:xxxiii+420pp. [No.2]
ISBN:1-56859-013-X(paper).